ENDORSEMENTS

"Sebastien Richard cleverly uses the collective likability factor of superheroes and brings the leadership values they model to the forefront for us to ponder and learn from them. If you don't want to lead like a superhero after reading this book, it's probably because you're a super villain."

CHRIS WIDENER,
author of *Leadership Rules*

"This book will make you look at superheroes, and leadership, in a whole new way. With Lead Like a Superhero, Sebastien Richard inspires us to go further, pushing us to meet the heroic versions of ourselves."

MEL ROBBINS,
bestselling author and motivational speaker

LEAD LIKE A SUPERHERO

What Pop Culture Icons Can Teach Us About Impactful Leadership

SEBASTIEN RICHARD

NEW YORK

NASHVILLE • MELBOURNE • VANCOUVER

LEAD LIKE A SUPERHERO
What Pop Culture Icons Can Teach Us About Impactful Leadership

© 2017 Sebastien Richard

Published in New York, New York, by Morgan James Publishing. Morgan James and The Entrepreneurial Publisher are trademarks of Morgan James, LLC.
www.MorganJamesPublishing.com

The Morgan James Speakers Group can bring authors to your live event. For more information or to book an event visit The Morgan James Speakers Group at www.TheMorganJamesSpeakersGroup.com.

Shelfie

A **free** eBook edition is available with the purchase of this print book.

CLEARLY PRINT YOUR NAME ABOVE IN UPPER CASE

Instructions to claim your free eBook edition:
1. Download the Shelfie app for Android or iOS
2. Write your name in **UPPER CASE** above
3. Use the Shelfie app to submit a photo
4. Download your eBook to any device

ISBN 978-1-68350-193-0 paperback
ISBN 978-1-68350-194-7 casebound
ISBN 978-1-68350-195-4 eBook
Library of Congress Control Number:
2016913952

Cover & Interior Design by:
Megan Whitney
Creative Ninja Designs
megan@creativeninjadesigns.com

In an effort to support local communities, raise awareness and funds, Morgan James Publishing donates a percentage of all book sales for the life of each book to Habitat for Humanity Peninsula and Greater Williamsburg.

Get involved today! Visit
www.MorganJamesBuilds.com

This book is dedicated to Edgar Richard, "Pépère," my grandfather.

Thank you for instilling in me the love of books.

You were a superhero to me.

CONTENTS

LEAD LIKE A SUPERHERO

ACKNOWLEDGMENTS

I would like to thank, first and foremost, my wife, Elisabeth L'Esperance Richard, for all the extra hours she had to put in taking care of our three young children, in addition to her coaching company (www.mindsetfuel.com) and housework, while I was in front of my computer researching and writing. I also want to thank her for her helpful advice, coaching, and constructive criticism, which helped in the advancement of this work. Liz, you are my toughest critic and my biggest fan—and I love you for it. You are truly a Wonder Woman leader.

Many thanks to David Hancock and the Morgan James Publishing team for giving a relatively unknown writer from the great white Canadian North a shot at being part of "The Published Authors' League," a unique group of superhero thought leaders ranging from Antiquity to our day.

Thanks to Angie Kiesling of The Editorial Attic (www.editorialattic.com) and editor Jennifer Hanchey, who edited and polished my manuscript and made it me—only better.

I would also like to thank Ryan Murphy for kindly providing me with DC Comics graphic audio books, which were not only great source material, but also just plain awesomeness for my mind. Ryan, I hope this book blesses you and adds value to your life.

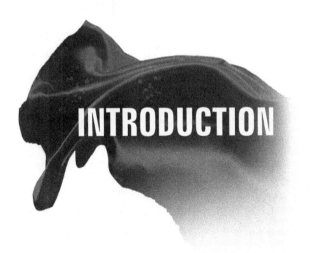

INTRODUCTION

I was four years old when my father first took me to see a movie on the big screen. For the occasion, I was lucky enough to see *Superman*, interpreted by the iconic Christopher Reeve. Seeing the Man of Steel take flight and save the world on the big screen as an impressionable kid left an undeniable impact on my psyche. As a boy, my first contact with a superhero was not only larger than life, but also inspirational, to say the least. I think what I found the most amazing, besides the fact that he could fly faster than a nuclear missile and change the course of a mighty river of burning lava, was his humanity. I mean, there was this guy, seemingly indestructible, letting out a soul-stirring scream and crying while holding the lifeless body of the woman he loved. That's what, as a child, had the most profound impact on me: how compassionate and caring he was—how human. It was his goodness that made Superman my favorite childhood hero. Of course, at the time, I would not have been able to explain it like this.

What is it with superheroes? Superheroes have become so influential in our culture today that the scope of their impact is now compared with that of Greek mythology! Of course, one could argue it's their cool superpowers that make them so popular. I have to disagree. While their superpowers make them super cool and beloved to us when we are young, it's their character that fascinates us when we are older. What makes us love them is not their powers, but rather how they employ them on a daily basis.

The complexity of how they interact with humanity, their loved ones, their allies, and their enemies, is what we love to see. Someone once put it this way: "Comic books are soap operas for men where a fight breaks out on a regular basis." Let's be honest, would Batman be so popular if we didn't know about his childhood trauma and how it affected every decision he made for the rest of his life? Let's face it; what we like about the Dark Knight is how he approaches a situation—and how he approaches a situation is linked to his psychological makeup. We like his character, his angle, how he goes about his business. We like who he is as much as what he does. Right? Absolutely!

I like what Aunt May says about heroes in *Spider-Man 2* (by director Sam Raimi). Peter Parker (Spider-Man) has quit being a hero and is visiting Aunt May. A kid by the name of Henry is helping her outside her home with some boxes. The boy asks Peter Parker about Spider-Man: where has he gone? Peter tells him the web-slinger has quit. Aunt May, saddened by the news, responds to Henry:

> Lord knows kids like Henry need a hero—courageous, self-sacrificing people—setting examples for all of us. Everybody loves a hero! People line up for them, cheer them, scream their names. And years later, they'll tell how they stood in the rain for hours, just to get a glimpse of the one who taught them to hold on a second longer. I believe there's a hero in all of us, that keeps us honest, gives

us strength, makes us noble, and finally allows us to die with pride, even though sometimes we have to be steady and give up the thing we want the most—even our dreams. Spider-Man did that for Henry, and he wonders where he's gone. He . . . needs him.

Wow! Needless to say, that little speech stirred Peter Parker to don the costume once again. Someone once said Peter Parker got his powers from the spider, but his strength from Aunt May. Her short speech epitomizes that courage. All this to say, Aunt May is right on when she says everybody loves a hero, that we need them. It's true. It was true for me growing up, and it still is. And when I look at my son, I see it's also true for him.

> "This book is about leadership as epitomized by familiar and beloved heroes. It's about what kind of leaders we are. It's about what kind of leader we should aspire to become."

This book is about leadership as epitomized by familiar and beloved heroes. It's about what kind of leaders we are. It's about what kind of leader we should aspire to become. In all my years of reading comics, I have found that much of what inspires me to be a better person can be found within the pages of DC and Marvel publications, among others. To paraphrase Jack Nicholson, super-heroes make me want to be a better man. And no, it's not because I have a crush on them. I know it may sound corny, geeky, or even naïve of me to say this, especially if you're a seasoned leader who might be reading these pages, but I speak the truth nonetheless.

Who can forget the famous line from Spider-Man: "With great power comes great responsibility"? Such lessons from comic books have become iconic in our culture—epic even! Many superheroes portray undeniably impactful leadership qualities. These qualities can be found in our daily lives—at home, at the workplace, and in our communities. And when we see those qualities operating in people, we admire them. These traits are universally recognized as being an integral part of what good leadership entails: strength, courage, intelligence, perseverance, compassion, self-sacrifice, etc.

Growing up, I learned a lot from these fictional characters. I learned lessons that enabled me to become a better son, brother, student, husband, father, employee, and citizen. The morals and values I read and observed from Superman, Captain America, and Optimus Prime, to name just a few, made me want to emulate those qualities in my own life. That's where superheroes transcend their medium (comic books, TV, movies). That's where they become cultural icons. I learned much about the value of self-improvement and discipline from Batman. I learned the importance of maximizing the strengths of others from Professor X. From Optimus Prime, I learned that "freedom is the right of all sentient beings." Those values are universal in their appeal. They know no bounds, and they only make us better.

So the purpose of this book is to look at the different leadership types of these heroes and make them applicable to our families, workplaces, communities, organizations, and places of worship—to our very lives. The heroes I will analyze in this book each portray very different leadership styles. They have their strengths, but also their weaknesses. They each bring a different leadership flavor to what I believe is a very colorful palette. My hope is that you will glean from these chapters what you may be like, who you might lead like.

Of course, no one leader is exactly like those I will describe at length. Your leadership style is probably a combination of two or more of those characters. You might be a bit of a loner like Wolverine and exhibit the compassion of Optimus Prime. If you're a woman, you may find you don't identify very much with Wonder Woman. Instead, you might find you exhibit the strategic smarts of Captain America. That's okay too. I'm not attempting to fit people into one category or mold. Leadership is organic. It's vibrant and alive. It's not static. That's what makes it so compelling, admirable, and invigorating.

Also, while you read, you will probably gain a lot of insight into what type of leadership approach works best in different situations. Not all situations require the same approach. Leadership from the front at full throttle, like that of Superman, might be good in many instances, but not all of them. Sometimes, a predicament will call for the analytical leadership from behind, like Batman's; other times, it needs the passionate, no-holds-barred, head-on approach of Wolverine. Always keep in mind that just as leadership is organic, so is life. One must learn to adapt and be flexible. Capacity to adapt and change is the greatest asset of intelligence, and what is leadership without intelligence?

Bruce Lee, who was as close to a real-life superhero as they come, described this flexibility:

"You must be shapeless, formless, like water. When you pour water in a cup, it becomes the cup. When you pour water in a bottle, it becomes the bottle. When you pour water in a teapot, it becomes the teapot. Water can drip and it can crash. Become like water, my friend."

In the same manner, *Lead Like a Superhero* is not intended as a stringent, biographical book about superheroes and their different leadership styles. So, if you're a fanboy and you picked up this book thinking it was strictly about the characters themselves, you might be disappointed. On the other hand, geeks (like me), fanboys, and, yes, even cosplay aficionados can apply the leadership principles in this book to improve their own leadership skills and become more than just fans of the genre. By modelling the principles in this book, many can become leaders and perhaps even heroes in their own right.

In fact, my deepest desire for *Lead Like a Superhero* is that it will inspire a younger generation of leaders to embrace the values modelled by the likes of Superman, Spider-Man, or Wonder Woman to better lead their own lives and the lives of those around them. These values are timeless and universal; they shape the character of the best men and women out there. In recent history, we witnessed just how much of the future is in the hands of those some would call geeks: think of Bill Gates and Steve Jobs. So if you're a self-proclaimed geek or fanboy and you are not sure if leadership is your forte, by all means keep reading.

Lead Like a Superhero is also a book written with self-improvement in mind. It is a book written for leaders or aspiring leaders, using leaders as examples. I could have written the same book using historical figures, like Napoleon or Abraham Lincoln. However, I felt it had been done before, and it's not what sparked my inspiration in the first place. All this to say, I don't want angry letters from fans who disagree with my views to flood my inbox. I had no intent to aim the content of this book uniquely to the comic book community, and I don't intend to have this book get me an invitation to speak at the next Comic-Con. Of course, I would not object to it (hell, no!), but that is not the primary goal of the book.

Also, as you will notice, the book only concentrates on positive leadership temperaments. I mean, we've all worked for either bad leaders or incompetent ones. However, I didn't see any value in adding supervillains to the mix. Catch my drift? Who cares how Magneto achieves his goals, right? And why waste time on why Megatron has devoted followers? And I will not expand on how Lex Luthor achieved financial success either. While there would be much to learn from a psychological point of view by analyzing the leadership styles of supervillains, I believe it would be too dark and lack inspiration. But, who knows? It could be material for another book someday. The psychology behind those characters could be interesting.

Now, I'm very aware that other books have been written on leadership and business with a superhero template. So what makes this book different?

Well, first off, I know superheroes very well. I am a fan, first and foremost. My love of the genre, as you will see, is infused throughout the book. I have read many articles online, and while there are books using superheroes as a template for leadership, most of them do it from an allegorical perspective. Their angle is more super-power focused than superhero focused. I think this hesitancy to use the characters themselves stems from the fact that they are fictional characters. Perhaps the writers fear bordering on the childish or ridiculous if they use the actual persona of childhood heroes as relevant and impactful leadership examples. Hence, they find it easier to tell us to "fly over our problems" or "use our minds like Batman" or "shield ourselves from bad thoughts." This is exactly what I didn't want to do.

I don't care if they are fictional or not; superheroes inspire millions of people around the world by who they are. Although fictional, they are as real as can be for the millions who flock to see them on the big screen every time Hollywood produces a new movie featuring them. The inspiration they light up in people's hearts, my own included, is as real and authentic as any real-life hero out there. I wanted to use this heartfelt connection as a launch pad. We all remember the popularity and positive impact of those WWJD (What would Jesus do?) bracelets back in the early 2000s. Well, although it never made the headlines, I know for a fact that many have also wondered "What would Batman do?" or "What would Optimus Prime do?" While those bracelets might never be manufactured, *Lead Like a Superhero* offers the next best thing.

Secondly, as I took on more responsibilities in life, I became a student of leadership. My responsibilities increased the further into manhood I moved. I came to understand and embrace the importance of becoming a better leader: to lead my family as a husband and father and to lead in my workplace and community. As I matured, I consciously made choices to know more about leadership, to read about it, to study it, and to apply it in all the spheres of my life. I strongly believe leadership begins in our own inner circle. So I didn't write this book only with corporate leaders in mind. I believe leadership flows from the heart, is strengthened in the mind, and begins at home. In this sense, it is almost a mental and spiritual martial art.

"I believe leadership flows from the heart, is strengthened in the mind, and begins at home. In this sense, it is almost a mental and spiritual martial art."

Thirdly, there are so many books out there that approach leadership from a buttoned-down, corporate, and, well, somewhat overly stern point of view. While some dimensions of leadership surely require much seriousness, I also believe powerful leaders need the ability not to take themselves too seriously. Getting insight from superheroes can bring much-needed freshness in the field of leadership books, especially for a younger generation of leaders.

Finally, as a man of faith, I strongly believe that God wants us to be good leaders, to demonstrate in our daily lives the noble qualities of superheroes and mighty leaders. Simply put, manhood (and womanhood) requires strong leadership, which I believe is severely lacking in today's world. So my faith was also a big factor in the writing of this book. Superheroes often exhibit the same qualities of biblical heroes. While biblical examples might not be the subject of this book, they have been an influencing factor. And if you're a woman, do not let the predominance of male heroes deter you from reading further. Leadership is not sexist, and we definitely need strong women out there who will be lights in a world of darkness. Because it's very much present, I have not forgotten the inspiration of women in comics. Nevertheless, throughout the book, gender-specific terms may be used in order to ease the text flow. Whenever a gender-specific term is used, it should be understood as referring to both genders, unless explicitly stated. This is done solely for the purpose of making the text easier to read, and no offense or sexism is intended. The only notable exception to this is the chapter on Wonder Woman. She is such a strong female character that I intentionally used her leadership example to empower women leaders out there. That is why you will find her to be portrayed as the only thoroughly gender-specific character. That said, you may be a dude and find you have a lot in common with her leadership style—and that's okay too.

If you're a leader, you will enjoy identifying and comparing your style with superheroes. This exercise will motivate you to lead better, identify the limits and weaknesses of your leadership style, and address any deficiencies. It will also inspire those who have not yet fulfilled their destiny as leaders to find their wings. It will also be an interesting read for any employee who is curious about the way his company is run. If you have a good boss, you might have wondered how he became that way. What makes him effective and likable? Finally, it will appeal to all who love leadership, comic books, and, yeah, good clean fun.

An apt elevator pitch for *Lead Like a Superhero* would be the following:

Lead Like a Superhero is an unconventional approach to leadership, perfectly tailored for a younger generation of leaders. It's an informative, fun, and inspiring new way to learn about leadership.

Or perhaps this one:

Lead Like a Superhero is a youthful and fresh approach to leadership that uses familiar heroes as a template. It's an invigorating and inspiring read that will make you want to ditch the suit and embrace the cape!

Whichever pitch you dig, these descriptors really put the book in perspective.

TIPS ON HOW TO READ THIS BOOK

In the following chapters, we will analyze the different types of leaders out there, based on the persona of well-known superheroes.

This is the part of the book where everybody will get what they want. Those who are reading this book because they love learning and deepening their knowledge of leadership principles will find it insightful and practical. Those who love comics and superheroes will find it a pleasurable and surprising read—and will gain leadership guidelines along the way.

Keep in mind that the descriptions accompanying each leadership type are generalized. It's not a one-size-fits-all analysis. I don't like to put people in boxes, and people generally don't like the confines of boxes either. That's okay. As you read the leadership types of the characters, you might find affinities with one of them, or three, or five. It's all good. People are organic; so is leadership. I wanted to make leadership facts fun, inspiring, relatable, and interesting.

For each character or "leader type," I give the following analysis:

CHARACTER BIO: The origin, powers, and persona of the superhero comprise his biography.

LEADERSHIP STYLE: How does this particular hero lead? As we look into the superhero's style of leadership, how do ordinary leaders who demonstrate similar qualities (leader types) compare? For example, how would an Optimus Prime leader lead in the real world? What characterizes these leaders? How can we recognize them around us?

STRENGTHS: What are the leadership strengths of the hero . . . and of the leaders who emulate him?

WEAKNESSES: What are the main leadership weaknesses of the particular hero . . . and the leaders who emulate him?

EFFICIENCY RATING: Every type of leader is given a report card for his effectiveness. This report card is based on eight leadership traits I believe are universally crucial to any leader; they are graded on a scale of one to ten:

PEOPLE SKILLS: The leader's know-how when it comes to communicating effectively, whether to an individual or a group. His capacity to gain trust quickly. His capacity for empathy. Basically, his EQ (emotional intelligence) and SQ (social intelligence).

SMARTS: The leader's keenness of mind, smarts, are his overall knowledge, quick wits, and IQ, paired with how and when to put them to good use. In short, smarts are the leader's acumen and know-how.

VISION: Vision is the leader's goal setting and scope. How far ahead is he able to see and make provisions for? How high is his aim and how functional is his plan?

CHARACTER: The leader's integrity and strength of character means doing the right thing, even when nobody is looking.

ADAPTABILITY: The leader's ease of adaptability and capacity to change gears when needed is his adaptability. Can he go to a plan B, C, or even D and rally his troops for the change?

FOCUS: Focus is the leader's drive and determination to reach goals. It is his capacity not to let trivial things derail him from priorities and to stay on track.

"IT" FACTOR: The leader's charisma enables him to gain trust quickly. The "it" factor is that *je ne sais quoi*, which brings that extra flavor to his leadership.

OVERALL: The leader's overall rating for his leadership quality.

CALL TO ACTION: What can we ultimately learn from the superhero? What should you do (like the said superhero) to better yourself and add to your leadership arsenal? In the end, isn't it all about doing? They're not called action heroes for nothing!

WHAT OTHERS HAD TO SAY: This section features fun, pop-culture-related quotes about the hero. These quotes are gathered from comics, movies, writers, and the actors who played the heroes. They give extra insight about the persona of the particular character.

As you will see, the heroes to make the roster have intrinsic leadership abilities, obvious from the comics and movies. They don't just exemplify one leadership quality or trait in particular. These characters are great leaders in their own right who have proven their mettle in a leadership role in the comics or on the big screen. They could come on board any organization and make a great impact as a leader. This ability is what I was looking for when I was writing *Lead Like a Superhero*. This is also why the roster is not overly extensive.

Every popular superhero did not necessarily possess the right profile. For example, you will not find the Hulk's profile listed. Or, sometimes, more than one character fit a certain profile, and I had to make a personal choice as to which to use. In the end, though, you will find these heroes cover the complete leadership spectrum we encounter in our lives and organizations. I believe all the gaps were filled, and I hope you enjoy reading the book as much as I enjoyed writing it.

CHAPTER 1

HEROISM AND LEADERSHIP

★　　★　　★　　★　　★

"The characteristic of genuine heroism is its persistency. All men have wandering impulses, fits and starts of generosity. But when you have resolved to be great, abide by yourself, and do not weakly try to reconcile yourself with the world. The heroic cannot be the common, nor the common the heroic."

—RALPH WALDO EMERSON

WHAT MAKES A HERO?

The dictionary definition of *hero* is, as follows:

he·ro ˈhirō/ *noun*, a person, typically a man, who is admired or idealized for courage, outstanding achievements, or noble qualities; "a war hero."

And the etymology of the word *hero*:

hero (n.1) late 14c., "man of superhuman strength or physical courage," from Old French, *heroe* (14c., Modern French, *héros*), from Latin, *heros* (plural *heroes*); "hero, demi-god, illustrious man," from Greek heros (plural heroes); "demi-god," a variant singular of which was *heroe.*

The late Christopher Reeve, a hero in his own right and a true Superman who inspired millions, also described a hero: "A hero is an ordinary individual who finds the strength to persevere and endure in spite of overwhelming obstacles."

> "A hero is an ordinary individual who finds the strength to persevere and endure in spite of overwhelming obstacles."
>
> # — CHRISTOPHER REEVE

Comic book legend Stan Lee put it this way:

Another definition of a hero is someone who is concerned about other people's well-being and will go out of his or her way to help them—even if there is no chance of a reward. That person who helps others simply because it should or must be done, and because it is the right thing to do, is indeed, without a doubt, a real superhero.

Logically, following this, one might ask, because of the context of this book, "What, then, is the definition of leader?" Well, here it is:

lead·er *noun*, the person who leads or commands a group, organization, or country; "the leader of a protest group."

Basically, if we were to boil it down, a hero saves and protects, while a leader influences, directs, and guides. But just how far do the similarities between the two terms go? After all, the definitions found in the dictionary do not seem to indicate much in common between the two. The website *History's Heroes* (http://historysheroes.e2bn.org) lists the different characteristics of a hero. How well do they compare to the characteristics a good leader should have? Well, let's see:

A hero is brave/courageous . . . so is a good leader.

A hero is a good and strong leader . . . so is a . . . well, duh!

A hero is altruistic (puts others' needs ahead of his own) . . . so is a good leader.

A hero is clever . . . so is a good leader.

A hero is a visionary (has far-reaching ideas) . . . so is a good leader.

A hero is good/moral . . . so is a good leader.

A hero has integrity . . . so does a good leader.

A hero is tenacious (keeps going despite challenges) . . . so is a good leader.

A hero is decisive . . . so is a good leader.

A hero is focused/single-minded (has a purpose) . . . so is a good leader.

A hero is inspiring/charismatic . . . so is a good leader.

A hero is determined . . . so is a good leader.

A hero is ambitious . . . so is a good leader.

A hero is wise . . . so is a good leader.

A hero is honest . . . so is a good leader.

A hero is kind/compassionate . . . so is a good leader.

A hero is just/fair-minded . . . so is a good leader.

Evidently, the traits that make us admire heroes are the same qualities that make for a good leader. Honesty, courage, virtue, decisiveness, perseverance, self-sacrifice, etc. There are, however, a few more distinctions to be made between the two terms.

A hero can act in a group or independently, while a leader's actions are always linked to group activity. Furthermore, a hero is automatically deemed good, while a leader can fall anywhere on the spectrum, based on the results he brings. One might say a hero rises through challenging circumstances where lives are at risk. A leader, however, can guide his followers through storms or fair weather and does not need to save lives to be effective. Leadership, unlike heroism, is a team sport—always. It is based on consistency and progress.

> ## "Leadership, unlike heroism, is a team sport—always. It is based on consistency and progress."

Heroism can be a five-minute act of selflessness that will be remembered forever. Not leadership. Leadership, in order to be deemed good, has to be tested through the long haul. A hero, when doing his deeds, always plays the role of a leader. A leader, however, when doing his job, does not necessarily play the part of a hero. So these are the major distinctions between the two.

Do you have the makings of a good leader or, better yet, of a hero? Well, if you believe in something good and you go at it in a way that helps others, then yes, you might just have the makings of a hero.

WHAT, THEN, IS A SUPERHERO?

What makes a hero into a superhero? A common definition of a hero says that a hero is one who knows to hang on just one minute longer. Well, a superhero will hang on one more hour, day, or sometimes even weeks. A hero might do one heroic act in his lifetime, while a superhero multiplies them on a daily or weekly basis. A hero can be an ordinary man or woman, while a superhero will exhibit strength, speed, intelligence, and fighting skills above human standards. A hero can wear a suit or jeans and a t-shirt; it just doesn't matter. A superhero usually wears, shall we say, more colorful attire. A hero can become a hero by acting unselfishly in the heat of the moment. A superhero chooses to act in heated moments day in, day out. They actually go looking for extraordinary circumstances. And we love them for it:

> We love our superheroes because they refuse to give up on us. We can analyze them out of existence, kill them, ban them, mock them, and still they return, patiently reminding us of who we are and what we wish we could be (Grant Morrison, from *Supergods: What Masked Vigilantes, Miraculous Mutants, and a Sun God from Smallville Can Teach Us about Being Human*).

So leading like a hero is one thing, but leading like a superhero means going that extra, grueling mile for the sake of others. It's being able to demonstrate superhuman endurance, empathy, and self-lessness. It means, like Joseph Campbell put it, "fighting for something which is bigger than oneself." And to that I might add, "with superhuman determination."

"Leading like a superhero means going that extra, grueling mile for the sake of others. It's being able to demonstrate superhuman endurance, empathy, and selflessness.

THE CULT OF THE HERO

Okay, this is the part where I get to admit to my geekiness. I don't know if my level of geekiness would qualify me as a bona-fide fanboy, but as the following anecdote will show, I'm pretty darn close.

I was into collecting action figures, especially Generation 1 Transformers. When I had been married for about three years, as luck would have it, there was a sci-fi and toy convention being held not too far from where I lived in Montreal. I made it my business to be there. Once there, I bought a couple of items but didn't want to go over the budget I had set for expenses that day. That's when I saw it: a vintage Generation 1 Snarl Dinobot. It wasn't in its original box, but it was really nice—no paint chip or scratches on it. It looked new and would make a great addition to my collection. As I kept admiring it, the owner noticed me and came in for the kill, er, the sale.

He was younger than I was, probably in his early twenties. As we began talking about how nice his Snarl figure was, I told him that, although it was fairly priced, I had already reached my budget. I told him my wife and I had agreed on a budget and she would be disappointed if I didn't respect it. That's when he gave me his pitch; it was truly genius.

"You have set a budget with your wife; I understand. This isn't any of my business, but how long have you been married?"

"Maybe three years or so," I answered.

"Are you guys planning on having kids?" he asked

I didn't know where this was going, but I was curious nonetheless, so I told him, "Yes, as a matter of fact, we are trying right now to start a family."

Then the conversation shifted.

"What did your wife play with when she was a kid?"

Before I could answer, not realizing it was a rhetorical question, he continued, "Chances are, she was playing mom with dolls or house with Barbies, right?"

"Um, yeah, my wife liked to play with dolls and Barbies."

"Are you guys homeowners now?"

"Yes, we are," I said proudly.

"So she played house, and lo and behold, today she lives in one. How do you think that makes her feel?"

"Well, good, I guess."

"And when she gets that first child, we could say that her childhood desire will be fulfilled. She will finally be giving life to that dream of becoming a mom, which is something many women dream of when they're little girls, right?"

"Right."

"So, basically, she will end up living out all of her childhood desires in real life—as an adult, no less."

He continued, "Now we, as little boys, dream of what? I'll tell you. We dream of being the hero, of saving the world, stopping the villains, and slaying the dragon. We dream of being Superman or He-Man or a G.I. Joe . . . Am I right?"

"Um, yeah. That's right."

"But what ends up happening? Do we end up doing any of that and fulfilling our deepest manly dreams? Do we get to kick the villain's a**, rescue the damsel, or save the world? No. We get to go to work—most of the time at a job we hate—and pay the bills, right?"

I sighed, "Yes."

He wasn't done. He continued, "So when we come to a convention like this, we basically try to get back a little of all those dreams we lost by indulging in our childhood fantasies. We try, through these hobbies and collections and action figures, to get a little bit of our manhood back. It's a bit sad and pathetic, but we don't live in the Middle Ages anymore. We don't get to be knights in shining armor. This is all we've got. This is our feeble attempt to keep the flame of heroism alive in our hearts."

He concluded by looking me straight in the eye and saying, "If I were you, I would buy this Transformer. Tell your wife that she gets to live her dreams on a daily basis—but you don't. And I would add that she shouldn't be the one to try to extinguish the flame of heroism in your heart because, deep down, it's what makes you a better man and husband. And then, I would tell her exactly what I told you in our little conversation."

Hook, line . . . and sinker! Yes, I bought the darn thing. Shameful, isn't it? This was, and still to this day is, the cleverest and smartest sales pitch I've ever heard. The guy knew collectible toys, but most of all, he understood the male psyche. He understood why we men admire heroes—and yes, I was a sucker for it. He understood what makes for this age-old cult of the hero. I know, deep down, he was just trying to make a sale. But, hey, it worked. Kudos to him.

Oh, and for the record, I sold all of my Transformers and action figures when my son was born. Don't judge me. I was broke and very much needed the money at the time. However, I didn't just do it because of the money we needed, but also because I felt I needed to. I felt I needed to aim for a certain level of maturity as a new dad, and selling was a way for me to reach a new height. Even though I don't own any more action figures, I'm still a fan. Case in point, this book!

HEROES AND MYTHOLOGY

"Superheroes fill a gap in the pop culture psyche, similar to the role of Greek mythology. There isn't really anything else that does the job in modern terms."

—CHRISTOPHER NOLAN

The DC animated movie *Justice League War* ends with Wonder Woman comparing the Justice League heroes to the ancient Greek gods. She looks at her teammates and says, "It was good to walk among the pantheon again." Superman quizzically asks, "What do you mean?"

And then she looks at all the members of the Justice League, who were all lined up, and ties each one of them to a Greek god: "Hades (Batman), Apollo (Green Lantern), Hermes (The Flash), Hephaistos (Cyborg), Zeus (Captain Marvel); each a god in their own right."

The comparison is actually quite striking. Their powers do actually compare very much with those of the gods of old. I guess this goes to say, there is nothing new under the sun. Heroes and their exploits have always fascinated us. They go waaaaay back. All the great civilizations and empires of history had their own unique pantheon of heroes and gods.

Even before Greek mythology, there were the gods of ancient Egypt and all the myths associated with them. And before that there was the Epic of Gilgamesh. And let's not forget Norse mythology (Odin, Thor, and Loki), still being used by Marvel Comics, along with Hades and Hercules borrowed from the Greeks. In fact, Norse mythology is actually making a comeback today. They are building "churches" dedicated to Odin in Europe as we speak. I don't know if the *Thor* and *Avengers* movies had anything to do with the resurgence of Odinism, but it is an interesting trend to say the least.

There is also the old Celtic and Welsh mythology from England, Scotland, and Ireland, which brought us the exploits of King Arthur, Merlin, Lancelot, and many others. Every epoch and civilization has their heroes and superheroes, gods and demi-gods. America, as today's influential global empire, is no exception.

Who knows? If the world is still around five hundred years from now, maybe future humans will look back on our civilization and say our pantheon of "gods" was composed of Superman, Thor, Batman, and Spider-Man. If someone in the far future were to find remnants of old comic books or the cover of the video game *Justice League: Gods Among Us* by DC Comics, what would he think? What would his conclusions be? Maybe this is just our modern twist on mythology and, in a way, part of our legacy and mythology as a people.

WHO IS YOUR HERO?

We all grew up with a hero or two we admired, whether fictional or real. As for myself, I gained wisdom and understood character by observing a few good men in my life. Growing up, I witnessed men whose praise never made it to the public eye, whose deeds were never recorded in books or in legend. Even so, they strived every day to do what was right and care for their families. They never let me down. Their steadfastness was remarkable to me and made a deep impression on my soul. These men and women are the Uncle Bens, Aunt Mays, and Alfreds of our lives, the Jonathan and Martha Kents of our daily grind. They are quietly heroic in the mundane. We need such people, ordinary people who selflessly act every day in such a way as to demonstrate integrity, perseverance, industry, and kindness. We need strong, intelligent, and compassionate men and women out there to show the way for younger people.

> We need strong, intelligent, and compassionate men and women out there to show the way for younger people.

We are truly blessed if we know courageous people, especially if they are our parents. Here is a wonderful poem titled *Only a Dad*, by Edgar Albert Guest, that epitomizes quiet heroism:

Only a dad, with a tired face,

Coming home from the daily race,

Bringing little of gold or fame,

To show how well he has played the game,

But glad in his heart that his own rejoice

To see him come, and to hear his voice.

Only a dad, with a brood of four,

One of ten million men or more.

Plodding along in the daily strife,

Bearing the whips and the scorns of life,

With never a whimper of pain or hate,

For the sake of those who at home await.

Only a dad, neither rich nor proud,

Merely one of the surging crowd,

Toiling, striving from day to day,

Facing whatever may come his way,

Silent, whenever the harsh condemn,

And bearing it all for the love of them.

Only a dad, but he gives his all

To smooth the way for his children small,

Doing, with courage stern and grim,

The deeds that his father did for him.

This is the line that for him I pen,

Only a dad, but the best of men.

Having been raised mostly by a single mother, I, perhaps, was on the lookout for those qualities more than most. I was hungry to witness traits in other men so I could emulate and model my own life after them. It was a deep and real need for me. I needed a hero, someone to look up to. So I gleaned much from comic book superheroes.

The writers of comics try to portray the best possible qualities in superheroes. These heroes not only move mountains (literally) and stop alien threats, but they are also top-notch men and women. They are not just superheroes, but super people as well. Although fictional, these characters demonstrate true valor, strength of character, and integrity. They can teach us more than a few things about strong leadership and good morals. Spider-Man and Superman, although fictional, were my heroes because they brought out the best in me. But, before we too can move mountains, we must learn to walk the daily grind, one quiet step at a time. We must learn to serve before we can lead.

"Before we too can move mountains, we must learn to walk the daily grind, one quiet step at a time. We must learn to serve before we can lead."

Aunt May told Spider-Man, "We all need a hero." It's true. I'm not the only one. We look for them everywhere. We seek them in our families, our communities, and in our entertainment. In fact, we especially seek them in our entertainment. Superhero and action movies always rank among the highest-grossing movies of any year. There is a reason for that. More than ever, people, especially young people, are looking for heroes, for people who put it all on the line to save others. In a world where integrity and selflessness are severely lacking, we are starving to see it. This is because we are in deep need for inspiration and leadership. Good leadership inspires us. John Quincy Adams said, "If your actions inspire others to dream more, learn more, do more, and become more, you are a leader."

Based on this definition, it can be said, without a doubt, many comic book superheroes, although fictional, are truly great leaders. In fact, I believe we can learn much of the character of a man by the heroes or superheroes he admires. Tell me who you admire, and I will tell you who you are.

YOUR LIFE IS EPIC

What made me a fan of superheroes in my teens and early twenties is hard to explain. Like most fans today, I suppose it provided me with an escape from the reality I sometimes (okay, often) found hard to bear. Of course, I fantasized about having Superman's powers, Iron Man's suit, or Batman's wit and money. But it was more than that; it was more than just fantasy to me. It had almost spiritual bearings on my personal growth. It appealed to my soul to such a depth that I have to wonder about the meaning of such fascination.

As human beings, I believe our life and purpose has deep meaning and that we play a much bigger part in the grand scheme of things than we like to believe. And as a man of faith, I believe that each and every one of us plays a part in a cosmic epic with a Master Director (God). I believe that when we are born, our birth has the effect of a pebble thrown in a pond. Like baby Superman hurled to earth on his Kryptonian ship, our arrival to earth is just as powerful. The ripples of our coming into this sphere of existence are far reaching. They affect others, time, space, and reality. I believe comic books and superheroes affect our culture so much because they serve to remind us of this powerful and deeply ingrained fact: we matter.

> "I believe comic books and superheroes affect our culture so much because they serve to remind us of this powerful and deeply ingrained fact: we matter."

Our story and our presence here matters. We are part of an epic story between good and evil, and guess what? Deep down, we know it. Superheroes and their stories merely remind us that we are a part of this too, that we can be heroic too. It's as if they awaken a faraway memory tucked away in our soul, perhaps a blurry vision of a possible future, a past rich in nobility, or a future in which we somehow know we will play a larger part. Comic books resonate with us because we wish to be part of something bigger than ourselves, something in which we matter, something special. The seeds of greatness and heroism are within us and beckon us to flourish. Comics and superheroes only serve to stimulate and remind us of our greater purpose and destiny.

In the comics or on the big screen, superheroes face threats and partake in events of epic proportion. They fight genocidal madmen, earth-shattering events, monstrous creatures with preposterous powers, wars, and alien invasions. They even travel through space and through dimensions to parallel earths! The adventures they live are simply mind-shatteringly epic. Not only do we dream of escaping the mundane but we, like our heroes, crave to be part of something special, grandiose, epic! And you know what? We are. You are. Dr. Steve Maraboli said, "If you are not the hero of your own story, then you're missing the whole point of your humanity."

Knowing this, we should all embrace our potential heroic greatness and make it flourish. Just as Joseph Campbell so aptly philosophised in his magnum opus *The Hero With 1000 Faces*, we must all embark on our hero's quest in this life. Like Paulo Coelho says in *The Alchemist*, destiny awaits those who pursue their own personal legend. And for those who dare to embark on this quest, superhero leadership is achievable through it. So, what are you waiting for? Ditch the suit and embrace the cape!

CHAPTER 2
THE DNA OF SUPER LEADERS

> *"We all have the capacity to be a superhero. In order to become one, you just have to find your unique power or ability and exploit it for the greater good. The cape and mask are optional accessories, but a kind heart is essential."*

—ROBERT CLANCY

Many different factors contribute to how superheroes exercise their gifts. In this chapter, we will examine the ramifications of superhero leadership from a psychological and emotional point of view and, yes, even from a spiritual one. These constitute superhero leadership building blocks or DNA, if you will. We will put superheroes under the microscope. Get your surgical gloves 'cause we'll open them up to see what's inside—what makes them tick. Ahem, er, I'm speaking allegorically of course. Otherwise, this would just be gross.

So what fortitude does one need in order to lead like a superhero? What is the mindset required? Why are there some leaders who demonstrate quiet strength and determination, while others are bold, loud, and in your face? Why are some leaders people oriented, while others are more task oriented? In short, what constitutes super-leader DNA? I'll give you a clue: it's 100 percent human DNA—not Kryptonian or otherwise.

Every superhero has a different style and different quality combinations that give him his own unique flavor. This is why heroes often go at it from different angles. They all bring something different to the table, yet they all lead and influence others in a positive way. As we will see in later chapters, when we put them even further under the microscope, every superhero, when leading, does so with his own characteristic flair and uniqueness. Nevertheless, there are essential DNA molecules without which there would be no leadership, much less superhero-quality leadership. I have classified these non-negotiables in three different groupings in this chapter:

1 *Mind and spirit*

2 *History and destiny*

3 *Heart and soul*

First: mind and spirit. What DNA molecules comprise the indomitable mind and spirit of a superhero? We will look at the three top qualities of a superhero leader's mind and spirit: his intelligence, his confidence, and his drive.

Second: history and destiny. How does a superhero's past influence his thinking and outlook? And how do a superhero's choices and leanings affect his present and future? And how does his leadership fare through it all? Our experiences, the company we keep, and our results are the key components linked with leaders' history and destiny.

Third: heart and soul. My favorite book says, "Guard your heart above all else, for it determines the course of your life" (Prov. 4:23). Wiser advice has seldom been given. A hero and leader's strength is measured by his heart. In this section on the heart and soul, we will consider how they are fortified by temperament, beliefs, and empathy.

1 THE MIND AND SPIRIT OF THE SUPER LEADER
THE HIGHER THE IQ, THE FURTHER THE VISION

"There are four ingredients in true leadership: brains, soul, heart, and good nerves."

—KLAUS SCHWAB

Notice how Mr. Schwab mentioned brains. Whether we like to admit it or not, intelligence is essential to effective and impactful leadership. Besides, have you ever seen a dumb superhero? Me neither. I've seen tons of stupid villains, though. Hmmm, I think we can learn something from that.

Anyway, the assertion that IQ is very important to a good leader is, surprisingly, controversial in today's prevalent leadership philosophy. Some would argue, perhaps in an attempt to level down and put everyone on equal footing, that IQ (quantitative intelligence) isn't really important to be an effective leader. They say character, insight, and determination—especially EQ (emotional intelligence)—is enough.

Well, I'm not too big on political correctness; therefore, I beg to differ. I have seen many enthusiastic, would-be leaders with great people skills who were very gifted in getting nowhere. Why? Well, to be bunt, they were just dumb. IQ acts as a compass that determines not only direction, but also the scope of your vision and helps you to plan appropriately to get there.

So this brings us to the age-old question: are leaders born or made? Although it may not be as clear-cut as "born or made," I do think some people are definitely gifted to lead while others just aren't. I'm very comfortable with that notion, even if some find it offensive. So no, I don't hold to the belief that just anybody can be a great leader. In my mind, that isn't true. I also believe we were all gifted with varying degrees of intelligence. Paul Okum, author of *Leadership DNA*, agrees with this notion:

> Leadership isn't the result of applying a formula; it is an expression of a person's own God given leadership talent or DNA, and it cannot be bestowed upon someone with a diploma.

That said, however, I do believe, and have witnessed in many instances, everybody can improve and work on developing leadership skills with proper discipline and training—even if he doesn't become a great leader in the process. We can all bring ourselves to a higher level. And science also proves that we can even raise our IQs. Isn't that good news?

To illustrate my point on the importance of IQ for leaders, let me ask you these questions: If you take away Batman's intelligence, what do you have? Just some guy in a bat costume. If you take away Tony Stark's (Iron Man) intelligence, what are you left with? Take away the suit, and he is still a "genius, billionaire, playboy, and philanthropist." But take away the genius, and you have no Iron Man, no money . . . nothing. And Spider-Man designed his web shooters (before his Hollywood incarnation) with his innate scientific knowledge; what is he without it?

Yes, intelligence is a defining factor in super heroics. The same can be said for everyday leaders. IQ really does make a difference in a leader's capacity and influence. It makes a great difference in the scope of his vision. And if not in his vision directly, at the very least in his planning and adapting to change. Capacity to adapt to change and chart a new course is a direct result of a leader's IQ.

It is important to note, however, that intelligence in leadership can now be categorized. The time when we believed IQ to be the only way to determine intelligence is over. We now have the aforementioned EQ (emotional intelligence) and more recently SQ (social intelligence), both of which are huge difference makers in leadership ability. In fact, many leadership experts say that EQ is the main difference maker in today's leadership ability ratings, more so than IQ. Warren Bennis, author and leadership expert, had this to say on the matter:

> Emotional intelligence, more than any other factor, more than IQ or expertise, accounts for 85% to 90% of success at work . . . IQ is a threshold competence. You need it, but it doesn't make you a star. Emotional intelligence can.

But how do we define EQ and SQ? EQ (emotional quotient) is a (notional) measure of a person's adequacy in such areas as self-awareness, empathy, and dealing sensitively with other people.

SQ (social quotient) is the capacity to effectively navigate and negotiate complex social relationships and environments.

Those were breakthrough findings in the fields of quantitative intelligence. There is even talk of advances in identifying spiritual intelligence as another area of study. So intelligence is multi-faceted. In the past, we knew of only two types: book smarts and street smarts. We've come a long way since then. I believe the best leaders are the most balanced between the many different strains of intelligence. A high IQ combined with a high EQ and a high SQ will make a superior leader compared to one who is only gifted with a high IQ. Empathy, compassion, and the ability to listen are tools of the trade of EQ, and they are absolutely necessary for effective leadership—just as much as IQ, which gives one the necessary know-how for planning and vision.

Now, as I mentioned earlier, the good news is that studies show IQ can be increased with regular reading and an increase in intellectual stimulation and "exercises." Even Alfred Binet, inventor of the IQ test, said, "With practice, training, and above all, method, we manage to increase our attention, our memory, our judgement and literally to become more intelligent than we were before." The same can be said of EQ. There are a variety of methods and habits that can increase one's emotional and social skills. Of course, like any self-improvement endeavor, it requires work, discipline, and consistency.

Questions: In what area do you think you should improve? Are you intellectually and emotionally adequate to lead? If not, what are you doing to increase your IQ, EQ, and SQ? There's always room for improvement, right?

NO CONFIDENCE, NO LEADERSHIP

I like what Batman says about Superman in *The Batman Files:* "He's not naïve, as I originally believed him to be. No, Clark is an optimist, raised to think that anything is possible and that any goal is obtainable. Not that much of a stretch for a man who can literally reach the stars."

Self-confidence—now there's something no superhero lacks. Given their levels of skill, power, and resources, this shouldn't come as a surprise. Of course, confidence is also crucial to good leadership among us mere mortals. The more you believe in yourself or your goals, the more convincing and trustworthy you will sound to others. You cannot sound convincing to others if you are not confident and convinced yourself.

But what does confidence consist of exactly? Simply this: self-confidence is our judgment of whether or not we can do something. It is a judgment call based on the weighing of all our capabilities—our abilities, our motivation, and the resources we can muster—versus the requirements of the challenge or task at hand. We make these assessments all the time, often unconsciously. We weigh ourselves, our capabilities, before important and unimportant activities in our daily lives. However, it is in our important activities that our confidence is truly tested.

Furthermore, self-confidence is, believe it or not, directly linked to how much an individual will have invested in his own personal development. For example, if on a scale of self-evaluation, you were to grade yourself as a three out of ten, it is likely a reflection of how much time and money you have invested in self-improvement. Highly confident people are people who have invested much in their own personal development. It builds confidence to build yourself up through personal growth. The more you invest in yourself, the higher you will grade your self-image.

> "It builds confidence to build yourself up through personal growth. The more you invest in yourself, the higher you will grade your self-image."

Keep in mind that leadership is, at its core, influence. And it is impossible to influence others without being confident yourself. John Maxwell put it this way: "When the leader lacks confidence, the follower lacks commitment."

Any discussion on leadership without addressing the issue of internal confidence in the leader is pointless. Now you may ask, "What about passion?" Passion and confidence go hand in hand. And in order to incite passion, you must first incite confidence. No one will be passionate on your team if you can't set a course for the future with confidence. "What about communication?" Would you listen to a leader who is unsure of himself, who lacks confidence? People naturally don't listen to those who are not sure of themselves. I sure wouldn't. "What about empowerment?" If you don't have the internal fortitude to make decisions and commitments, then empowerment is just a big word. You cannot empower others if you are not empowered first in your own mindset. No guts, no glory. Confidence is the crucial corner stone in leading like a superhero. If you want to be a strong leader, then you must pour a rock-solid foundation of self-confidence.

Every now and then, whether in comics or on the big screen, we will be shown a story arc in which the superhero loses his powers. Whenever this happens, what becomes of the hero? He becomes sullen and loses his, that's right, confidence! And when he loses his confidence, what becomes impossible? Pretty much everything. It's a simple equation really: confidence = influence = victory. There is no leadership or influence or victory without confidence. Just ask any superhero who lost his powers.

Now the good news is there are plenty of ways one can boost his self-confidence. The mind can be programmed to serve us, or it can be programmed to handicap us. It's our thoughts that ultimately affect our behaviors. This capacity to shift our mindset and ultimately change our behaviors is called neuro-linguistic programing. It is basically the ability to change our behavior patterns through auto-suggestion. Energy flows where focus goes. This process is what Dr. Maxwell Maltz coined "psycho-cybernetics" in his excellent book, which bears the same name. I highly recommend it. Always keep in mind, it's never too late to change your mind.

WHAT DRIVES YOU?

"A man's worth is no greater than his ambition."

—MARCUS AURELIUS

Many of us have heard the slogan that success is not about what you drive, but what drives you. I'll be candid here. For the longest time, I had very little or no ambition. This was partly because of a dysfunctional childhood, but also because of a negative perception of the word itself. I believed ambitious people were, like the definition of the word indicates, "striving for favor, courting flattery; a desire for honor, thirst for popularity."

As a Christian, I thought this mindset unbefitting. I believed myself to be humble by avoiding it. My mindset was wrong, and it needed to change. Thankfully it did when I finally understood this concept espoused by Napoleon Bonaparte: "Great ambition is the passion of a great character. Those endowed with it may perform very good or very bad acts. All depends on the principles which direct them."

You can be ambitious to feed the hungry or to rule the world. You can be ambitious to make more money so you can help more people, or you can be ambitious to make more so you can gloat and live large.

The worth and value of your ambition hinges on the principles which nourish it.

"The worth and value of your ambition hinges
on the principles which nourish it."

Needless to say, my low-ambition mindset in my twenties contributed negatively to my well-being and overall success. It took me years of self-improvement to finally "get it." We are what we think of ourselves; we become what we think. While I didn't think much of myself, I wasn't much. Oh, I had much to offer. I was well read and perfectly bilingual—and not too bad looking. But I had no ambition because I didn't believe in myself. You see, self-confidence results in ambition, and ambition determines our drive, how driven and pro-active we are. It's only when I changed my thoughts that I was able to put my drive in overdrive. That's when I truly began living life for the better and flourished.

If you look around at the great leaders in this world, you'll notice they all have this in common: they are very ambitious and driven; they are all about forward motion. Just like superheroes, they too are action heroes. It's only when I got fed up of tipping the scale between average and mediocre that I decided to do something about it. Ambition is born when you realize and believe you can do better, and you resolve in your heart and mind that you will. It's a decision to go all out. Leaders are firm believers in self-improvement and practice it on a daily basis. Your desire and drive to become better will determine how good you actually become. Superheroes are ambition driven. They are ambitious to bring peace, security, inspiration, and hope to a world that needs it.

2 THE HISTORY AND DESTINY OF THE SUPERHERO LEADER

Superhero backstories are critical. They define the "why" of the character. They make us understand why he embraced the cape and/or mask, and they make us understand the reason for the hero's unique style, approach, and personality. In the same way, our history has a lot to do with who we are today. Our circumstances and subsequent choices have brought us to the here and now. We are the product of those two very crucial factors. Our history and destiny are intertwined. Where we come from influences the choices we make, and the choices we make will determine where we'll ultimately be going.

EXPERIENCES WILL GREATLY DETERMINE HOW YOU LEAD

"What is the secret of success? Right decisions. How do you make right decisions? Experience. How do you gain experience? Bad decisions."

—ABDUL KALAM

Whether we like to admit it or not, much of what we are is the sum of our experiences and how we reacted to them—our decisions. And for the most part, our bad experiences had more to teach us than our good ones. Our past, the good and the bad, has shaped us into who we are today. Our experiences often determine the level of our maturity, provided we are able to process them properly. And herein lies the key, as we will see.

Always remember that leadership is organic. As such, it is malleable. For that matter, we are organic as human beings and, therefore, very malleable by our circumstances, especially in childhood. Comic book writers know just how much this is true. This is why they very often use origin stories to mold their character's personality. So not only will your past determine how you fare as a leader, but it could also determine if you lead and how well you do it. Let's consider how the past has shaped some of our favorite heroes.

Captain America and Optimus Prime were both kind-hearted weaklings who were given instant power and abilities through science. I like what Captain America says about weak men (his past): "Why is someone weak? Because a weak man knows the value of strength, the value of power." Optimus Prime was Orion Pax, a simple dock worker who, after being critically wounded by Megatron, was rebuilt into the wise and powerful Autobot leader. They are two leaders who, because of their past, know the value of strength and use it wisely. This is virtue.

Batman and Spider-Man suffered the loss of loved ones early on. Bruce Wayne saw his parents murdered before his eyes. Peter Parker lost his parents and later could have prevented the death of his beloved Uncle Ben. Later in their lives, they experienced loss yet again: Batman lost Robin (Jason Todd) and Spider-Man lost the girl he loved (Gwen Stacy). Both vowed to act in ways to prevent losses to others. They know just how much the loss of loved ones can hurt. Preventing similar suffering shaped their lives. They have chosen a life of responsibility, no matter the cost. It is what drives them. This is discipline, a vocation even.

Wolverine and Oracle suffered great physical ordeals. Wolverine was experimented on by his own government and endured torture at the hands of wicked men. Barbara Gordon was crippled by a merciless act of the insane Joker and chose to become Oracle. These two both know that the wicked shouldn't go unpunished.

They know firsthand what evil lurks in the hearts of men. They had to overcome many demons, and still they fight on the side of angels. This is dedication.

Superman and Wonder Woman have quasi-divine origins. Superman was hurled to earth in a spaceship as his home planet blew up, like some sort of messiah. Diana has divine origins (whether divinely given life from clay or daughter of Zeus . . . take your pick). They are two of the most powerful beings in the superhero world and have chosen to embrace the values of compassion, sacrifice, and altruism. With their almost god-like powers, they could have chosen to be worshipped, yet they chose to serve mankind instead. This is humility.

Of course, there are a myriad of other defining circumstances and difficulties comic book superheroes have been through since their origin stories. Heck, Superman, Captain America, and Optimus Prime even died and came back to life! Other heroes, not profiled in this book, also had a turbulent past. Barry Allen (The Flash) lost his mother when he was ten years old. Martian Manhunter (a member of the Justice League) lost his family and his whole civilisation in a terrible war. Bruce Banner (The Hulk) grew up with an abusive father who killed his mom. Yeah, that would piss me off too. I don't know if I would turn green and start tearing up cities, but I would definitely have some pent-up anger issues concerning my past.

The point is, the power of such experiences to shape a leader's mindset and perspective is huge! And this massive impact, depending on your character, can tilt the scale towards either fruitfulness or barrenness. It depends on the leader's response to his experiences. Let me explain. Just as experiences can make us stronger, they can also paralyze us, causing us to cower and retreat from facing life. The event can make us fearful of having another similar trial, which in turn causes us to play it safe. Some of us, after getting our bumps and bruises, decide not to venture out and take risks anymore. Just like Hulk, we run to the desert and "want to be left alone." But good leadership must involve risk, right?

In order to develop as superhero leaders, we must be mindful in how we respond to our life passages, to our experiences. In the end, whether in comics or in life, we have two types of likely leaders forged through experience:

1. Leaders who responded poorly to life's hardships: These leaders develop faulty worldviews and mindsets. This makes them lead out of fear or pride. It can make them paranoid and bring them to abuse their power. As I'm sure you know, "fear is a path to the dark side." Those who do not overcome their past trials will try controlling others and will seek position as a means to exert influence—just like your boss. This is how supervillains lead, by the way. Yeah, I'm kidding . . . or am I?

2. Leaders who responded well to life's hardships: These leaders face their trials from a learning stance, looking for opportunity and lessons to be learned, remaining open, vulnerable, and teachable. These men and women lead authentically. Their leadership is not from pride. They exert influence through relationships, character, and commitment. Enter superhero leaders, like you, perhaps.

The process in which leaders use their life experiences to shape who they are is described by Warren Bennis in *On Becoming a Leader:*

Until you make your life your own, you're walking in borrowed clothes. Leaders, whatever their field, are made up as much of their experiences as their skills, like everyone else. Unlike everyone else, they use their experiences rather than being used by it.

So, what leadership qualities has your past forged in your heart? How do you use these qualities in your family, workplace, and community? Think hard and deep about your past—what gems have come from it? Likewise, what flaws stem from your past? What corrective measures should you take to correct them?

Superhero leadership is about growing and learning continuously, and then giving back. A leader who stops growing and learning from his past, no matter how hurtful it was, will inevitably lead poorly. Hindsight will give you insight on your past. And with that insight, you are more valuable as a person, a leader, a human.

> "Superhero leadership is about growing and learning continuously, and then giving back."

SUPERHEROES ASSEMBLE!

"Avengers assemble!" With this one cry, Captain America summons the willingness of (arguably) the greatest superhero team ever to work together time and again. With this one rallying shout, they always put aside their differences and join together to fight for something greater than themselves. As a team, they are far more powerful and effective than they ever would be alone. The guidebook to the supernatural (i.e., the Bible) gives us this direction:

"Do not be deceived: Evil company corrupts good habits"
(I Cor. 15:33, NKJV).

"As iron sharpens iron, so a man sharpens the countenance of his friend"
(Prov. 27:17, NKJV).

There is no denying the powerful influence of the company we keep. Our friends and family act as a sculptor's scissors on our persona. Human beings are born imitators. They model one another, for better or worse. There are three types of people in our lives: the ones we are given (our families), the ones we choose to let in (our friends), and all the others. Ultimately, the people we spend the most time with will greatly influence the person we become, the leader we become. The late Jim Rohn is well known for saying, "You are the average of the five people you spend the most time with." That's exactly right. And here is what you will find: mediocre people will want you to be mediocre; average people will want you to be average; and great people will want you to be great. I find this a fascinating observation of human behavior. People will want you to remain on their level. This is why we should surround ourselves with great people.

"Ultimately, the people we spend the most time with will greatly influence the person we become, the leader we become."

Most superheroes of comicdom have a fairly good family background. And when I say good, I don't mean perfect. I mean they were raised by good and decent people. Think about it. Where would Superman be without the loving care of Jonathan and Martha Kent or Bruce Wayne without Alfred or Peter Parker without Uncle Ben and Aunt May or Optimus Prime without Alpha Trion?

It's undeniable that much of who we are was implanted very early in life by our caregivers. Chances are, the better they were, the better we are. Of course, I say this as a general rule. Some had rotten parents/caregivers yet became very decent people; others had great parents/caregivers and became rotten human beings. Nevertheless, all in all, the influence and nurture of our parents and family is a powerful force that can potentially make or break us.

As for the other people in our lives, luckily, we get to choose them—well, our inner circle anyway. Superheroes are lucky because they generally hang out with one another; they sharpen each other's leadership skills. They are, generally speaking, high achievers and good quality people. They rub off on each other. They each benefit from that inner circle greatly. I, for one, tried to enroll in The Avengers for that same reason, but I failed the entrance exam. Captain America's handshake at the start of the interview had me crying uncle. That was the end of it.

"Life chooses your acquaintances, but you must choose your friends. My advice: choose wisely!"

Yup, ordinary people like you and me do not benefit from such a great entourage. We have to choose our friends wisely. I once read somewhere that life chooses your acquaintances, but you must choose your friends. My advice: choose wisely!

Leadership entails teamwork. Leadership expert John Maxwell put it well: "One is too small a number to achieve greatness. No accomplishment of real value has ever been achieved by a human being working alone."

Only super beings can achieve greatness alone—and last time I checked, you and I can't fly. So, yes, it is essential for any leader to develop encouraging friendships, to surround herself with the right kind of people. The people surrounding you will either make or break you. They can make you better or make you worse. And, be careful if you are surrounded by average people. This can trick you into believing that everything is fine and that you shouldn't seek better people. If you believe your friends to be good people, it could prevent you from seeking out better or great people. Only great people can make one rise to greatness. Stagnation is the enemy of achievement, and it is often the subtle result of being surrounded by average people.

Captain America makes The Avengers great because he is great, and vice-versa. Batman, Superman, and Wonder Woman make the Justice League great because they are great—they constantly challenge one another to excel and to improve. Also, I believe in having an inner circle filled with people whose strengths are different from yours, whose assets complement your own. On a team, if everybody is good in the same areas and weak in the same areas, there will be very little progress. For example, if you're not very computer savvy, it would really help your team to have someone who is. Or if connecting at a deeper level with people is not your forte, maybe someone else is very gifted in that area and can pick up your slack. Our different strengths are what make a strong team.

Make an inventory of your surroundings. How is the quality of your relationships? Do the people around you challenge and inspire you? Do you look up to them? Do they look down on you? Someone once said, "If you are the smartest person in the classroom, you're in the wrong classroom." Is it time to change classrooms?

RESULTS INDICATE LEADERSHIP CAPACITY

*"Effective leadership is not about making speeches or being liked;
leadership is defined by results not attributes."*

—PETER DRUCKER

Trial and error, adjustments after failures, and accolades after successes all affect how we will lead in the future. Our successes and failures
set the tone for our future results. Leadership is very pragmatic. It is
very much defined by results and momentum. A leader's results will
increase or damage his confidence level, his reputation . . . and his
future results.

Positive results will inevitably:

★   Build momentum

★   Increase self-confidence

★   Increase your level of influence

★   Increase your credibility

★   Increase the trust of your followers

★   Secure your reputation

And, of course, negative results will bring the opposite and may,
in fact, disqualify you as a leader altogether. I like how superheroes
get results. They will not only save the day and vanquish the villain,
but they do it in such a way as to minimize civilian casualties in the
process. They don't want any innocents to get hurt while they trash
the bad guy—and sometimes the city. It's always in the back of their
mind, even when they hurl a car at their enemies. They aim, as much as
possible, to get results in a way that inspires trust from the population.

"Over time, I have come to this simple definition of leadership:
Leadership is getting results in a way that inspires trust."

—STEPHEN COVEY

3 *THE HEART AND SOUL OF THE SUPERHERO LEADER*

In the first *Spider-Man* movie, starring Tobey Maguire, Norman Osborn, Spider-Man's nemesis, was musing to himself how to hit the hero where it hurt the most. The Green Goblin, Osborne's alter ego, evilly echoed in his deranged mind: "The cunning warrior attacks neither body nor mind . . . The HEART, Osborn! First, we attack his heart!"

Indeed, the heart is where it's at. This is where true strength and valor comes from. From your heart and soul rivers of life flow. This is where passion and dreams are born. It is the essence of everything each of us are—the good and the bad. It is the deep furnace where leaders are forged.

TEMPERAMENT AND LEADERSHIP

I contend that it is of the utmost importance, in order to be a good leader, to know yourself. Socrates, when he coined the Greek aphorism, "know thyself," hit the nail on the head. I hate to break it to you, but you can have a mountain of knowledge in many disciplines, but if you fail to know yourself, you wasted years of your life on trivial stuff.

Another Greek, this time Hippocrates, contributed a great deal to medicine and also to the field of self-knowledge when he came up with the four basic temperaments over twenty-four hundred years ago:

> The Greek physician Hippocrates (c. 460–c. 370 BC) incorporated the four temperaments into his medical theories. Four temperaments is a proto-psychological theory that suggests that there are four fundamental personality types, sanguine (optimistic and social), choleric (short-tempered or irritable), melancholic (analytical and quiet), and phlegmatic (relaxed and peaceful). Most formulations include the possibility of mixtures of the types (Wikipedia).

Although the theory that four basic temperaments govern the personality types of people has somewhat faded in popularity, I have found, through personal study and social observations, most people—and superheroes for that matter—do fall in these categories, with a blend of one dominant and one subordinate temperament. I can easily recognize those temperament blends in most people. When you are well versed in those four temperaments, it is quite easy to surmise another's type; it's amusing even. Moreover, I have found that the study of personality is a really great way to know thyself.

So here, for your benefit, is the lowdown of the four basic temperaments and how they relate in the field of leadership.

Sanguine

The sanguine are usually called "super-extroverts." This temperament is usually thought of as a "natural salesman," but they enter many professions suited for those who are outgoing, such as acting, for example.

They "lead into a room with their mouth" and are never at a loss for words. They love being the center of attention, and if you're throwing a party and you want it to be a success, invite them. Their outgoing nature makes them the envy of the more timid temperament types. They are most comfortable around people and do not like being alone. They get a charge off people. They are often known as "touchers," reaching out and touching the arm or shoulder of the person they are talking with.

Their high energy can make them seem more confident than they actually are and their cheery disposition often cause others to excuse their weaknesses by saying, "That's just how he is." The sanguine are mostly happy people whom others enjoy having around. Inactivity causes them stress because the pace at which they like to live their lives is fast and furious. The sanguine are the most impulsive of all the temperaments. They often say yes before they think things through. Think: Tony Stark (Iron Man), Spider-Man (not Peter Parker!), or Deadpool (the mercenary with a mouth).

Sanguine leaders possess the following strengths:

- ★ Volunteer for jobs
- ★ Think up new activities
- ★ Look great on the surface
- ★ Creative and colorful
- ★ Have energy and enthusiasm
- ★ Start in a flashy way
- ★ Inspire others to join
- ★ Charm others to work

And the following weaknesses:

★ Would rather talk

★ Forget obligations

★ Don't follow through

★ Confidence fades fast

★ Undisciplined

★ Priorities out of order

★ Decide by feelings

★ Easily distracted

★ Waste time talking

Choleric

This temperament is identified as the most "powerful" and most leadership-oriented of the temperaments. The Latin word *cholericus* is where the French word *colérique* comes from, which means angry. Cholerics are the movers and shakers of our world and often occupy positions of leadership in the work force. They are extremely tough-willed, and they can be quite stubborn. They seek to have total control over themselves and their environment. Cholerics are of the opinion and belief that they know what is best for those around them, what is acceptable behavior. Oh, and don't make them angry . . . you wouldn't like them when they're angry.

People of choleric temperament possess multiple strengths:

★ Strong leadership leanings

★ Dynamic and active

★ Compulsive need for change

★ Must correct wrongs

★ Strong-willed and decisive

★ Unemotional

★ Not easily discouraged

★ Independent and self sufficient

★ Exude confidence

And the following weaknesses:

★ Bossy and impatient

★ Quick tempered

★ Enjoy controversy

★ Come on too strong

★ Unemotional

★ Domineering

★ Impatient

★ Rash

★ Manipulative

★ Demanding

★ Workaholic tendencies

★ Know it all

Their motto is usually "do it now." And they do get it done. They are good at planning and are often practical and solution-oriented. They appreciate receiving respect and esteem for their work, but then again, don't we all? Think: Wonder Woman (without the weaknesses) and, yeah, The Hulk, but not for any leadership qualities. Catch my drift?

Extroverted personalities: the choleric and sanguine personality types are more out-going, sociable, and comfortable in a crowd, even standing out in a crowd. Their leadership style is naturally more driven and people oriented.

Melancholic

I once read that the melancholy personality is the richest of all temperaments, but at the largest cost. History would probably reveal this to be true. Melancholy personalities are people who have a deep love for others, while usually holding themselves in contempt. For example, if ten people complimented the work of a melancholy and one person criticized it, a melancholy would lose sleep over the criticism, rather than be encouraged by the compliments. They tend to be deep thinkers and feelers who often see the negative attributes of life, rather than the good and positive things. They are very susceptible to melancholy (hence the name) and depression. They feel too much. The saying by Horace Walpole sums them up well: "Life is a comedy for those who think, and a tragedy for those who feel."

Melancholies are the most dependable of the temperaments, due to their perfectionist tendencies. Their analytical abilities allow them to accurately diagnose obstacles and problems, which often keep them from making changes. They prefer the status quo and may often seem overly pessimistic in their outlook.

Melancholies may choose a difficult life vocation involving personal sacrifice. Some may choose to become doctors, or scientists, or artists . . . or superheroes. They tend to be almost manic perfectionists, which can impede their decisiveness. They also are usually dissatisfied with themselves and are highly self-critical. Think of Captain America, who has all the strengths of a melancholy leader, without the weaknesses, and also Batman. However, those two are most accurately described as a combination of both melancholy and choleric temperaments.

Melancholy leaders generally possess the following strengths:

* ★ Schedule oriented

* ★ Perfectionist, high standards

* ★ Detail conscious

* ★ Persistent and thorough

* ★ Orderly and organized

* ★ Neat and tidy

* ★ Economical

* ★ See the problems

* ★ Find creative solutions

* ★ Need to finish what they start

* ★ Like charts, graphs, figures, lists

And the following weaknesses:

* ★ Can be socially awkward

* ★ Depressed over imperfections

* ★ Choose difficult work

* ★ Hesitant to start projects

- ★ Spend too much time planning

- ★ Prefer analysis to work

- ★ Self-deprecating

- ★ Hard to please

- ★ Standards often too high

- ★ Deep need for approval

Phlegmatic

People with this temperament may be inward and private, thoughtful, reasonable, calm, patient, caring, and tolerant. They tend to have a rich inner life, seek a quiet, peaceful atmosphere, and be content with themselves. They tend to be steadfast, consistent in their habits, and thus steady and faithful friends. Their speech can be slow or appear hesitant. The calm, peace-loving phlegmatic normally does not flock towards leadership positions. They usually prefer a more low-key role in any organization. However, when they do rise to a position of leadership, their super-sharp minds tend to compensate for their apparent lack of "take charge" attitude. They are often scientists, accountants, or medical practitioners. Think of Dr. Bruce Banner, Charles Xavier (Professor X), Reed Richards, Peter Parker, and Clark Kent.

Phlegmatic leaders generally possess the following strengths:

- ★ Highly intelligent

- ★ Competent and steady

- ★ Peaceful and agreeable

- ★ Administrative ability

★   Mediate problems

★   Avoid conflicts

★   Good under pressure

★   Find the easy way

★   Reliable

★   Loyal

And their weaknesses are:

★   Not goal oriented

★   Lacks self-motivation

★   Hard to get moving

★   Resents being pushed

★   Lazy and careless

★   Discourages others

★   Would rather watch

★   Complacent

Introverted personalities: the melancholic and phlegmatic personality types are more shy and reserved and can generally feel anxious about being in a crowd, especially at being singled out in a crowd. Their low-key leadership style is more task oriented as they generally prefer dealing with projects and things rather than with people. But they do excel at it.

So, did you recognize yourself in those temperaments? Would you be able to pinpoint your dominant and subordinate temperaments?

As a young man, I studied these temperaments and took a personality test. I was classified as a blend of 60 percent melancholy and 40 percent sanguine. This rang very true with my own nature at the time. As I've grown older, however, the negative qualities of the melancholy have somewhat faded, and I now have more of an upbeat and positive nature, which has greatly helped me in my relations with others and my work. As my negative outlook faded and as I gained more self-confidence, my sanguine side came out more. Today, I believe myself to be more sanguine, although my wife would probably disagree.

All this to say that temperaments affect our choices. But our choices, relationships, and circumstances can also affect our temperaments. Consider Peter Parker, also known as Spider-Man. Before he was bitten by a radioactive spider, the teenage lad was very studious and even a bit of a recluse (a definite phlegmatic). His new powers changed much of that. When he donned the suit of Spidey, he then became very talkative, humorous, and confident—more like a sanguine. His circumstances changed his outlook, and, in turn, his temperament was affected, even improved. He went from being a low-confidence introvert to a highly confident extrovert.

The other heroes in this book can also be classified by identifying their temperaments. The one problem, however, is that they have achieved such a high level of leadership and excellence (in most cases), that their temperament's weaknesses, which should also serve to identify them, do not shine though as much as they would in normal people. Also, like most of us, they exhibit a combination of two temperaments: one dominant and the other subordinate.

Take Wonder Woman, for example. She definitely demonstrates the strengths of a choleric, but very little, if any, of the weaknesses. For instance, she is actually quite compassionate, which is not the strong point of most cholerics. We do not, however, encounter the same problem with Batman. He is a very identifiable choleric, warts and all, combined with a subordinate melancholy. Or is it the other way around, as mentioned previously? In any case, his temperament combination shines through in every decision and action he takes.

In Captain America, Optimus Prime, or Superman, who are the most gifted in terms of strength of character and leadership qualities, we find a combination of most of the qualities found in all four temperaments, with almost no weaknesses (kryptonite doesn't count here).

Some heroes appear more flawed. For example, Marvel, more so than DC Comics, has made it one of their trademarks to willfully portray their superheroes as flawed human beings. This is a smart marketing move since it makes their heroes somewhat more relatable to the public at large. Wolverine fits that bill perfectly. His temper (choleric) and his brooding (melancholy) are quite easy to spot. Spider-Man, when created by Stan Lee, was meant to be "a superhero with problems." This was revolutionary at the time. And let's not forget Tony Stark's (Iron Man) drinking problem.

> "Your temperament will dictate if you are more task or people oriented, if you like thinking or acting, the risks you are willing to take, and even if you prefer following or leading."

Well, to sum it up, temperament definitely affects leadership style. Your temperament will dictate if you are more task or people oriented, if you like thinking or acting, the risks you are willing to take, and even if you prefer following or leading. What is your temperament combination? You can find out here:

http://temperaments.fighunter.com/?page=test

Or use Google to find a test version you like. It's interesting, fun, and will help you know yourself better, which can only help you grow as a leader.

YOUR BELIEFS WILL DETERMINE YOUR METHODS

"We do not act according to what we know; we act according to what we believe." I heard this on TV once, and it struck me as a bit off at the time. However, upon careful pondering and through my own personal experience, I have realized this statement was absolutely spot on!

"Your beliefs will affect your actions and ultimately your destiny."

Consider the wisdom of Gandhi:

Your beliefs become your thoughts,

Your thoughts become your words,

Your words become your actions,

Your actions become your habits,

Your habits become your values,

Your values become your destiny.

In short, your beliefs will affect your actions and ultimately your destiny. For example, Batman tends to believe that few people can be trusted. Living in a city full of psychopaths, freaks, and murderers has made him quite paranoid, understandably so. How does that paranoia influence his leadership? Not for the better. The Dark Knight actually knows this about himself. He understands his own major flaws. He matter-of-factly admits his deficiency:

If Clark wanted, he could use his super speed and squish me into the cement. But I know how he thinks. Even more than the kryptonite, he's got one big weakness. Deep down, Clark's essentially a good person . . . and deep down, I'm not.

In a story arc, which DC used to make an animated movie called *DOOM*, Batman analyzes all of the members of the Justice League in order to identify their weaknesses and determine a way to beat them. Why? Well, he figures if they ever were to lose control of their phenomenal powers and turn to the "dark side," such information would be vital to neutralize them. Needless to say, when the team finds out, they are very upset. And to make matters worse, they find out because this information had fallen into the hands of the Legion of Doom, enemies bent on destroying the Justice League! Oops.

Another example of this principle is how superheroes and supervillains perceive humanity. I have often heard there is a very thin line that separates being good from being evil. In comics, how one perceives humanity could be that thin line. Superman, Spider-Man, Optimus Prime, and most superheroes perceive humanity as worthy to be protected, because they see the good in man.

Obviously, the same cannot be said of Megatron, Dr. Doom, or Ra's Al Ghul. They see humanity as a cancer that should be annihilated or enslaved for the achievement of their goal. They see mankind as unworthy vermin, wicked and vile. Therefore, the destruction of the human race is no big deal to them. Their beliefs about mankind determine the direction of their leadership and action plans. While most heroes would gladly die to save humanity, the villains perceive humanity as an obstacle on their path to glory.

These attitudes and beliefs can also be found in leaders from our workplace and other organizations. Those with a sense of entitlement will inevitably lead others poorly. Those with a genuine concern for their fellow workers will lead them with respect and care. They will also tend not to ask employees to do something they wouldn't be willing to do themselves.

Ultimately, what we believe about ourselves will affect how we lead others. Have you ever heard the saying, "People will not care how much you know, until they know how much you care"? To be honest, this is something I had to learn the hard way. And I still struggle with it. Putting others' needs before our own is done only when we make it a part of our belief system. We might agree and nod to this principle intellectually. We might know it to be true. But if we do not believe it, we will not apply it. The knowledge that is in our heads has to be digested and go down to our hearts. The difference between head and heart knowledge is the same as that between knowledge and wisdom. A lot of knowledge, without wisdom, will be applied poorly, if at all.

EMPATHY IS A POWERFUL MAGNET

Empathy:

★ Seeing with the eyes of another

★ Listening with the ears of another

★ Feeling with the heart of another

Therefore, empathy does not require superpowers. You do not need X-ray vision to see from another's point of view. Super hearing is not a requirement to understand what another has understood. Empathy is all about heart, compassion, and a genuine concern for others—to understand them and put yourself in their shoes. Knowledge is the currency of the mind; empathy is the currency of the soul.

"Knowledge is the currency of the mind;
empathy is the currency of the soul."

To be honest, this is something I have had to work on quite a bit—and still do. I can be a self-centered jerk at times. Yeah, I own up to it because I understand that it's also part of being human. We generally tend to be self-centered creatures; it's human nature. It takes true humility and maturity for us to genuinely care about others, to put their needs ahead of our own. But here's the thing: you cannot lead others if you do not have empathy. Oh, you can have all the leadership skills in the world, but if you lack empathy, the end result will be that no one will follow you. Like the African proverb says, "He who thinks he is leading and has no one following him is only taking a walk." Others will only follow when they know you care.

I have found that empathy is like a muscle; the more you use it, the stronger it becomes. Empathy raises the standard of our leadership ability. It also raises the level of trust that emanates from others around you. Personally, I wouldn't trust a leader who doesn't care for me. This is mostly why the superheroes of comics are such good leaders: they care! And the more they care, the better leaders they make. The same goes for us folks without superpowers. Fortunately, we don't need powers to be empathetically strong.

EVOLVING YOUR LEADERSHIP DNA

Although superhero leadership DNA might not have been provided to all in the same measure, it is nonetheless something everybody has some measure of. And fortunately, the organics of leadership DNA permit evolution and change in our leadership skill levels.

- ★ Our temperament can be improved through knowledge, volition, or circumstances.

- ★ Our experiences can be harnessed and evaluated, in hindsight, to better ourselves.

- ★ The company we keep can always be changed and improved upon.

- ★ Our confidence can be increased through positive reinforcement and a growth mindset.

- ★ Our beliefs can be altered through our point of view.

- ★ Our intelligence can be increased with certain brain exercises or by adding to our vocabulary through reading more.

- ★ Our ambition can be channelled and determines how far we'll go.

- ★ Our results can improve if we improve.

- ★ Our empathy and altruism can be extended; as far as our words are heard, our hands will reach, and our feet will go.

> "Progress is the way of a true superhero leader. Always aim to do better, to become better, to become more than you are today, and to grow. Always strive to do the best you can."

We are not set in our ways. Our evolution as leaders hinges on choice and intentionality. Change is not only possible but necessary. Progress is the way of a true superhero leader. Always aim to do better, to become better, to become more than you are today, and to grow. Always strive to do the best you can. So as you surely figured out, the purpose of this rather long chapter was twofold: to know yourself and to grow yourself. That's superhero DNA evolution in action.

"If you make yourself more than just a man, if you devote yourself to an ideal and if they can't stop you, you become something else entirely—legend, Mr. Wayne."

—RA'S AL GHUL

CHAPTER 3

THE SUPERMAN

THE LEADER WHO FORGES
AHEAD LIKE A LOCOMOTIVE

"You're much stronger than you think you are. Trust me."

—SUPERMAN

CHARACTER BIO

Faster than a speeding bullet, stronger than a locomotive, able to leap . . . ah, you know the rest. And if you don't, what planet have you been living on? Superman is the most iconic of all superheroes. He's larger than life. He's the whole package. He fights for truth, justice, and the . . . all right, so he's not into politics anymore. Still good, right?

Since he first came on the scene in 1938, Superman has demonstrated some of the best qualities one would want in a leader. He is strong, courageous, intelligent, and self-sacrificing. He's even an icon of masculine handsomeness!

Most of us are very familiar with Superman's unearthly origins. He hails from the planet Krypton and was sent to earth on a rocket ship by his father (Jor-El) before his home planet became unstable and blew up. Under earth's yellow sun, he developed phenomenal superpowers, which include vast super strength, super speed, flight, super-hearing, heat, telescopic and X-ray vision, and freezing breath. And yet, in spite of his phenomenal powers, Superman has often faced threats so big that his very life was in danger. He has put it all on the line on many occasions in the comics and on the small and big screens—even dying at the hands of a creature called "Doomsday" while defending Metropolis and the world back in the early 1990s and in the recent *Batman vs. Superman* movie. That says a lot about the character of Jonathan and Martha Kent's (his adoptive parents) boy.

Some would argue that Superman is a little too "bread and butter" as a hero. I've heard it said that he's just too squeaky clean and proper to be interesting as a character. Well, in some ways, he is—but in a good way. Because of his good deeds, he has been deemed the world's biggest Boy Scout. Not many superheroes would take the time to rescue a cat out of a tree. There is even a psychological condition named after him! According to Wikipedia, the Superman complex is "an unhealthy sense of responsibility, or the belief that everyone else lacks the capacity to successfully perform one or more tasks. Such a person may feel a constant need to 'save' others." It was coined by Dr. Fredric Wertham in his controversial 1954 book *Seduction of the Innocent.*

In Big Blue's defense, though, I find it unfair to accuse him of being somewhat boring. If we analyze his background, it is actually admirable that Clark Kent chose to live his life the way he has. I was once musing to myself what I would have done if I had been given his powers. I certainly would not have chosen to become a newspaper reporter. Nope. I mean, a newspaper reporter, even a great one like Clark Kent, will not earn much more than, oh, say, eighty thousand a year—even taking into consideration that he works for a big metropolitan newspaper like *The Daily Planet*. And keep in mind that Clark sends a big chunk of his paycheck to help out Martha, his widowed mom in Smallville, Kansas.

Call me egotistical, but if I had been given these superpowers, I would have chosen the career of an athlete in pro sports. Being a hockey fan, I was thinking along the lines of an NHL goaltender. I even have a plan to stay under the radar: just let a few goals pass you by throughout the year to not let any suspicion arise. A great NHL goalie will post a goals against average between 2.00 and 2.50. To make sure I would be an all-time all-star, I would just maintain myself between 1.00 and 1.75. This way, you rewrite the record books, laugh all the way to the bank, AND you even get to wear a mask to keep your identity hidden! But enough about me and my silly fantasies.

What sets Clark apart is his desire not to stand out, but to blend in. He is so confident in his powers that he doesn't even worry about money. And if he ever does get short on cash, he doesn't resort to stealing or "cheating" by raiding a diamond mine or something either. No. This, in a way, is what makes Supes so admirable: he doesn't use his powers selfishly. He doesn't even use his X-ray vision on the ladies. He's a true gentleman and demonstrates exemplary self-control. This mindset is due, in large part, to his adoptive parents and his wholesome upbringing. Many times, whether in the comics or on the big screen, Jonathan Kent would remind Clark not to use his powers to be flashy or selfish. In many ways, Clark has been raised with very old school, all-American, traditional values. Although an alien, he is as American as apple pie.

LEADERSHIP STYLE

While being admirable, noble, and almost beyond reproach, the leadership style of Superman is, without a doubt, that of an overachiever. Can you blame him? I mean, the guy has almost god-like powers! In the superhero realm, he is the closest thing to being omnipotent and omnipresent. All he has to do is fly in space and lend an ear downward to earth to hear all the cries for help of humanity. He can fly from America to Australia in thirty seconds or less. The things he can accomplish in one single day are astounding. Such powers are sure to influence the approach and methods of the Man of Steel.

But what about the men of steel in our families, workplace, communities, and organizations? Are there leaders, human leaders, who demonstrate, on a daily basis, the leadership qualities of Superman? Or course there are. These are the people who are driven, energetic, and smart; they get things done—a lot of things! Whether we call them overachievers or super achievers, these leaders know the way, show the way, and forge ahead. They are the locomotives of the corporate world. They have a never-say-die attitude, nerves of steel, and a high-energy personality. They always look at a situation positively. Why? Because they are confident that, no matter how dire a situation is, there are no hopeless situations, just hopeless people. They also have high confidence in their own abilities. I have sometimes looked at such leaders in awe, thinking, "Where does he get all this energy?" For all I know, maybe they are Kryptonian. Because what they get done is often out of this world! The Superman-type leaders are so strong and driven that many of them have changed our world.

Examples of Superman leaders are George Washington, who, like Superman, could not tell a lie. And, of course, many parallels have been woven between Jesus Christ and Superman's origin story. In just three years of ministry, the Nazarene changed the world; even our calendar was changed forever (BC and AD)! The world was never the same after he showed up.

STRENGTHS

The strengths of Superman leaders are obvious. Of course, they don't have heat vision or freezing breath, but sometimes they make you wonder. I know some of them have super speed. They have numerous enviable leadership qualities, such as strength of character, high energy levels, intelligence, multiple talents, people skills, integrity, and know-how. They are charismatic movers and shakers. They are early risers (often before the sun) and work long days. They are also hard not to love. Most of the time they are very likeable and upstanding people, which makes them appreciated by the people they lead. Due to their positive outlook, they have a way to uplift and encourage others with their words. The glass is always half-full with them. In fact, even if it's empty, they already see what the glass will look like when it's full. These leaders are, without a doubt, beyond reproach and the top men and women of our organizations—but they are not perfect.

WEAKNESSES

So what is the kryptonite of the Superman leader? Do they have weaknesses? Of course they do; everybody does. To sum up their major weakness, I'll use a quote from the comics. In the January 1972 issue, *Superman* #247, Superman is given the notion by the Guardians of the Universe that he might be holding back social progress on earth by his presence, which makes him think:

> For years, I've been playing big brother to the human race. Have I been wrong? Are they depending on me too much, too often? Maybe I have been interfering unnecessarily. I decide what's right or wrong and then enforce my decision by brute strength.

And in the JLA/Avengers crossover published in 2003, it was made clear throughout the storyline that Superman worried he did too much at times. Which brings us to this point: do Superman leaders do too much and spread themselves too thin? The answer is yes. They are so gifted and energetic that they fail to delegate to others who would be well suited to help. I suppose that's where the Superman complex comes into play. It's not that they don't trust others (like Batman leaders, more on that later), it's just that they don't think they need the help. Also, they want to do it all for the sake of others. They think that's their way of being serviceable or efficient. Of course, this can be easily remedied if it is acknowledged, which can only help their overall effectiveness.

EFFICIENCY RATING

Back in 1993, in the wake of Superman being killed off in the comics, Saturday Night Live did a skit in which superheroes gathered to say a eulogy for the Man of Steel. I remember The Flash, obviously depressed, said something like this: "Superman could do anything, he was fast, strong, and had all these powers. Me, all I can do is run fast."

Yes, Superman leaders can seemingly do it all. Because of their vast array of skills and competence, Superman leaders have great overall efficiency. They are capable of operating on a high level in many different situations and with many different people. Just like the many superpowers tool box of the comic book character, they offer incredible versatility. They are multi-talented super achievers who bring a lot to any organization. Just as Superman is the ultimate superhero, Superman leaders could be deemed as the ultimate leader type. Superman leaders appear stronger than a locomotive. They can change the course of mighty corporations and are able to leap over tall problems in a single bound. Their rare combination of business savvy, charisma, and people skills make them a rare and valuable find for any organization.

PEOPLE SKILLS: 10

SMARTS: 9

VISION: 10

CHARACTER: 10

ADAPTABILITY: 10

FOCUS: 10

"IT" FACTOR: 10

OVERALL: 10

CALL TO ACTION: BE A SUPER ACHIEVER

Over the years, we have seen an evolution in how great accomplishments are wrought. We have gone from the term overachiever, which had the negative connotation of a dabbler and burn-out, to super achiever, which is seen in a positive light. What is the difference, you ask?

Overachievers do too many things and spread themselves too thin—unless they're really Superman. Super achievers do fewer things with greater results. They channel their talents and skills into what they do best. They focus their strengths and use their time and energy to yield the greatest results for themselves and their organization. One project + 100 percent focus = super achievement. And then they move on to the next project with that same focus. Super achievers go from one success to another because they do not tackle too many things at once. In fact, they know if they can just focus on one thing, it will be better than attempting two. And two is better than three, and so on.

"One project + 100 percent focus = super achievement"

A lot has been said in recent years about the extra-special fictional superpower of multitasking. Well, I hate to be the bearer of bad news, but here is what I think of multitasking: if you don't have Superman's superpowers, you will suck at it. Period. Super achievers are the antithesis of multitaskers. But even with his incredible powers and capacity to multitask, Superman had to learn to focus. In the movie Man of Steel, we see a young Clark Kent experiencing his budding powers in school. He had some kind of breakdown due to a power surge and panicked. His mom had to talk to him through the broom closet door in order to calm him down. She did this by helping him to focus, to channel his powers. He thus learned greater efficiency. In the same manner, we all need to learn to focus.

Dr. Jim Loehr, a world-renowned performance psychologist, co-founder of the Johnson & Johnson Human Performance Institute, and author of sixteen books said, "There's no such thing as multitasking." And Bosco S. Tjan, Professor of Psychology at the University of Southern California said, "Most of the time multitasking is an illusion. You think you are multitasking, but in reality you're actually wasting time switching from one task to another . . . If you are working on two things at once, you have to get the first thing out of your memory before you work on the next one. So you're switching in and out." Or, in the words of a *Facebook* meme I saw on the subject, "Multitasking means screwing up several things at once." Multitasking on a grand scale is what most overachievers do. On the other hand, super achievers single-task projects . . . and they crush them!

In Superman's case, his senses are so finely tuned and powerful that they border on precognizance. His vision powers are so potent that he can almost see things before they happen. In the same manner, super achievers are so focused on the one thing that what they accomplish transcends human understanding. Stephen DeVore said it best in this observation:

> I noticed an almost universal trait among Super Achievers. These people knew what they wanted out of life, and they could sense it multi-dimensionally before they ever had it. They could not only see it, but also taste it, smell it and imagine the sounds and emotions associated with it. They pre-lived it before they had it. And that sharp sensory vision became a powerful driving force in their lives.

If you are focused and determined, you can all accomplish a lot more in a day than you think you can, one task at a time. You can be a super achiever.

WHAT OTHERS HAD TO SAY

"It is a remarkable dichotomy. In many ways, Clark is the most human of us all. Then . . . he shoots fire from the skies, and it is difficult not to think of him as a god. And how fortunate we are that it does not occur to him."

—BATMAN

"I remember the first time I met Superman. It was a Justice League case so there were other heroes involved, but in my mind none of them stood as tall or as proudly as Superman. I began to wonder what I was doing in the same room as him, how little he must think of me. But Superman never treated me as anything but an equal. At six inches tall, he made me feel like a giant. Now I had to be that giant for him."

—THE ATOM

"I remember the first time I met Superman. Barry was going to introduce us. I was just standing on the rooftop, watching Barry talk to Superman. I must have tapped my foot a thousand times, fighting the urge to ask for his autograph. I started to get down on myself looking at him—like I could never measure up. I felt like taking off my costume and walking away. When they finished talking, Superman walked over to me, put his hand on my shoulder, and said, 'I wish more young people were like you.' Afterwards, I couldn't stop smiling for a week."

—THE FLASH (WALLY WEST)

"What makes Superman a hero is not that he has power, but that he h as the wisdom and the maturity to use the power wisely. From an acting point of view, that's how I approached the part."

—CHRISTOPHER REEVE, ACTOR

"*If I had to choose a superhero* to be, I would pick Superman.
He's everything that I'm not."

—STEPHEN HAWKING, THEORETICAL PHYSICIST AND COSMOLOGIST

CHAPTER 4

THE SPIDER-MAN
THE SELF-SACRIFICING
SERVANT LEADER

★ ★ ★ ★ ★

"With great power comes great responsibility."

—SPIDER-MAN

CHARACTER BIO

S pider-Man is one of the most recognizable and popular superheroes in the world. The "web-slinger," as he is often called, was created by Stan Lee and first appeared in *Amazing Fantasy* #15 (cover dated August 1962, on sale June 5, 1962). And the rest, as they say, is history.

Most of us know the origin story, of how awkward teenager Peter Parker was bitten by a radioactive spider and afterward developed phenomenal spider-like abilities. He found himself suddenly able to cling to walls, had enhanced strength and amazing acrobatic agility, a spider sense which warns him of danger . . . and a bit of a cocky attitude.

In addition, most of us are also familiar with the consequences of this cocky attitude. By neglecting to stop a petty thief after a wrestling match, he failed to stop the death of his beloved uncle, Ben Parker. The thief in question shot his uncle only a few minutes (or days, depending on the origin story) after Peter Parker didn't bother to stop him. It was this carefree mindset that Peter Parker was so remorseful over. It was this tragic event that defined the kind of superhero young Peter Parker would become: the Amazing Spider-Man! His motto became, "With great power comes great responsibility." It was a hard-learned lesson, indeed. Being self-serving had a huge price tag for Parker, a heartbreaking one. This explains why the young man did a 180-degree turn and became one of the best servant leaders in the superhero community.

Spider-Man is also defined as a superhero with problems. Stan Lee, when he created him, was intentional about that. He wanted young people to identify with him because his life was complicated. Peter Parker must juggle his job as a photographer for the *Daily Bugle*, his relationships, and his great responsibility as Spider-Man. He has known money problems and relationship problems; he has suffered loss many times. In spite of all of this, he keeps going, donning the mask to stop criminals and super-powered freaks. The story of Spider-Man is very much one of daily self-sacrifice.

LEADERSHIP STYLE

"With great power comes great responsibility." Those few choice words have echoed not only in comic books, but across the landscape of pop culture as well. They have inspired countless youths (and some not so youthful) to strive in the face of difficulty and keep going in spite of seemingly insurmountable odds. They have strengthened and exhorted many tired souls. These forceful words define, not only the actions of Spider-Man, but the actions of great leaders everywhere. They are, at their core, words of self-sacrifice.

Spider-Man's leadership style is all about self-sacrifice. He was going to use his newfound powers to make it big in the entertainment industry, until what befell his Uncle Ben. That's when his mindset shifted, from carefree and money oriented to responsible and self-sacrificial. And when I say self-sacrificial, I mean it. His commitment to responsibly using his powers has caused him to give up many comforts and suffer injustice such as:

★ Having a hard time holding on to a job

★ Experiencing bumpy relationships with his girlfriends

★ Weathering cash problems

★ Being maligned in the newspapers and media

★ Grieving and losing loved ones (his first girlfriend, Gwen Stacy, died at the hands of the villain Green Goblin)

★ Having those he cares about put in danger

★ Suffering sleepless nights

★ Accumulating more bumps, cuts, and bruises than he cares to remember

Yet, despite all of this, watching Spidey at work, you would never know about his trials. He always seems so carefree, and he's always cracking jokes. When he dons the suit, the rather timid Parker turns into the class clown. You can see he really enjoys his powers.

Okay, so his commitment to doing what is right is obvious, but what about leadership? Is Spider-Man really a model of leadership? Isn't he a bit young or immature? When you look closer at this amazing superhero, the answer couldn't be clearer. Is he a leader? The answer is a resounding YES! Here is why:

★ He does what is right, even if he doesn't get credit or if it puts him in danger.

★ He always puts the needs of others ahead of his own (even if it means not getting the job or the girl, or even losing friends).

★ He always does his best.

Just think for a second about those three defining characteristics and imagine how impactful they would make any leader out there. Yeah, now you're getting it. You see, we dismiss Spider-Man as a leader because he doesn't have much to show for it. Spider-Man is definitely a winner when it comes to stopping supervillains. He always finds a way to beat them, and he's very resourceful. Nevertheless, he's a mere teenager, always cracking jokes, and his results in his personal life are subpar. But this perception isn't fair. Sometimes, albeit exceptionally, a leader's results do not reflect his capacity. The exception confirms the rule, right? In all honesty, the Spider-Man style is probably the one I identify the most with. But that's just between us, okay?

If you make him lead a project and shoulder the load, he will get it done. Usually, however, this will take a toll on him. The Spider-Man leader is usually younger than his peers and, as such, often prefers to serve as second in command of a group. Their dedication to be responsible and their willingness to self-sacrifice make them an invaluable cog in any organization. Their overall commitment and gifting also makes them up and coming among their peers. We see how valuable Spidey's contribution is in Marvel's *Civil War* comic book epic; both sides want him to tilt the scale in their favor. Spidey is portrayed as the wild card in the conflict. By the way, you should treat yourself to the Graphic Audio rendition of *Civil War*, it's much better than the movie and really portrays Spidey in this way– it's pure fan candy.

Another thing that defines the leadership of Spider-Man, or the Spider-Man leader, is that leadership doesn't have to be buttoned down and serious all the time. It can also be youthful and fun. Yes, you read that right; leadership can be fun! In fact, I believe it should be. Being light-hearted and cracking jokes, even when doing a very serious task, can have a wonderfully calming effect on uptight meetings or stressed-out employees. Of course, discerning when and how to use such humor is an art that not everybody should engage in. But for the Spider-Man leaders who have a knack for it, it just makes everything more enjoyable and positive.

STRENGTHS

Most of the strengths of the Spider-Man leader flow from his heart. The Spider-Man leader is strong because he cares. He's kind, good natured, fun, easy going, and self-sacrificial. He always thinks of others first. He leads by serving. Spider-Man leaders are also highly intelligent and intuitive. They are very humble. They don't care about who gets the credit as long as, at the end of the day, everything is well with the world (or their employees, company, organization).

I was once watching a Spidey cartoon on TV in which he was working alongside other less-experienced superheroes. When their actions were careless and they almost caused innocent civilians harm, Spider-Man took them aside and reprimanded them saying, "We have superpowers; they don't. Remember that." That's the epitome of the Spider-Man leader—always looking out for those under his care.

WEAKNESSES

Oftentimes, Spider-Man leaders are younger and more inexperienced. This makes them more impressionable. They tend to look up to more seasoned leaders. This trait isn't bad per se, but it can make it difficult to see themselves as leaders. When they do this, they are blind to those looking up to them. This lack of self-knowledge and confidence in their abilities can impede their efficiency in leadership positions. Don't get me wrong. They are able, but they don't always believe they are— hence the problem. Younger Spider-Man leaders can also be quite sensitive to criticism. Also, their wisecracking sense of humor can sometimes make others not take them seriously.

EFFICIENCY RATING

The humility and capabilities of Spider-Man leaders, combined with their willingness to serve and self-sacrifice, make them surprisingly effective and amazing even (pun intended). They care and operate at a very high efficiency level. They are often the go-to people when employees need to be empathically understood. Servant leadership is the hardest attitude to master for most leaders. A leader who has harvested this particular skill can grow most others from this one.

PEOPLE SKILLS: 9

SMARTS: 10

VISION: 7

CHARACTER: 10

ADAPTABILITY: 10

FOCUS: 8

"IT" FACTOR: 8

OVERALL: 8

CALL TO ACTION: BE A SERVANT LEADER

Servant leadership is a timeless concept, but the term "servant leadership" was coined by Robert K. Greenleaf in The Servant as Leader, an essay he first published in 1970. Any respectable teacher on leadership will endorse servant leadership as the truest and most efficient leadership trait. I am no exception. I would never listen to any self-help or leadership expert if the principle of servanthood did not appear throughout his teachings. Leadership is not self-serving; it is simply serving. Spider-Man does it every day when he swings into action. It's his "why."

"Leadership is not self-serving; it is simply serving."

In an article on servant leadership, Dr. Kent M. Keith identified four key elements of servant leadership:

1. The moral component, not only in terms of the personal morality and integrity of the servant leader, but also in

terms of the way in which a servant leader encourages enhanced moral reasoning among his followers, who can, therefore, test the moral basis of the servant leader's visions and organizational goals;

2. The focus on serving followers for their own good, not just the good of the organization, and forming long-term relationships with followers, encouraging their growth and development so that over time they may reach their fullest potential;

3. Concern with the success of all stakeholders, broadly defined—employees, customers, business partners, communities, and society as a whole—including those who are the least privileged; and

4. Self-reflection, as a counter to the leader's hubris.

These are the worthy aims espoused by servant leaders everywhere. One common misconception for many aspiring (green) leaders is that you can't lead if you're serving. Get it straight: serving others doesn't mean that you are not leading. In fact, just the opposite is true. The greatest leaders in history are those who became servant of all. Are politicians and cops not defined as public servants? Granted, many have lost sight of that, but it's true nonetheless. Spider-Man leaders everywhere remind us just how much magnetism and charisma stems from servant leaders. Their empathy and altruism is very attractive. We want to follow them because we know they care, period. While Spidey has a "spider-sense," they have a "servant sense" and always go out of their way to help others by properly identifying others' needs and addressing them.

If you're a leader, do you expect to be served, or do you make it a priority to serve? Servant leadership is one of the most important, yet somewhat misunderstood, leadership principles ever taught. Well, it is misunderstood only for those who do not understand the true nature of leadership or for those who want to abuse it. Any leader worth his salt will attest to it as being indispensable. It's even one of the most famous teachings of Jesus Christ:

Whosoever will be great among you, let him be your minister; And whosoever will be chief among you, let him be your servant: Even as the Son of man came not to be ministered unto, but to minister, and to give his life a ransom for many (Matt. 20:25-28, KJV).

All this is to say that servant leadership is nothing new. It's not a modern teaching or principle—and it certainly isn't just a trend. At its core, it is the epitome of genuine leadership and always has been. If you want to be a great leader, be a servant to all. Is it easy? Hell, no! Is it worth it? Absolutely! You'll get out of it more than you will ever put in. It is the most efficient way for a leader to get compound interest on his efforts. That's why Spider-Man still does it. Because he has found that there is, indeed, more pleasure in giving than in receiving.

WHAT OTHERS HAD TO SAY

"Spider-Man's probably my favorite. You see, Batman is a billionaire, and there's nothing really cool about a billionaire saving the world. But Spider-Man is Peter Parker, a conflicted character who puts on a suit and saves the world. I love that."

–ZAC EFRON, ACTOR

"What's cool about Spider-Man is that it's everybody—anyone, you put on the suit, anyone believes that you're Spider-Man. That's what's charming about the character. He's anyone. He's a huge nerd that ends up being this huge superhero."

—JAKE EPSTEIN, ACTOR

"Spider-Man has always been a symbol of goodness and doing the right thing and looking after your fellow man."

—ANDREW GARFIELD, ACTOR

"I never thought that Spider-Man would become the worldwide icon that he is. I just hoped the books would sell and I'd keep my job."

—STAN LEE, CREATOR OF SPIDER-MAN

CHAPTER 5

THE BATMAN
THE LEADER WHO LEADS FROM THE BACK, ANALYZING

"It's not who I am underneath, but what I do that defines me."

—BATMAN

CHARACTER BIO

Batman is by far the most fascinating and complex superhero. He is, arguably, the most popular and the one with the greatest appeal. Born from the imagination of Bob Kane back in 1939, Batman quickly established himself as a superhero like no other. Young Bruce Wayne's dark and tragic past contributes to the complexity of his psychological makeup.

After seeing his parents killed in a dark alley, young Bruce Wayne resolved to avenge them by making sure criminals would never hurt other innocents. He chose to instill fear in this cowardly and superstitious lot by donning a bat costume and waging war on Gotham city's lowest of the low. To achieve this, he travelled the world to train with the best of the best, honing his skills in all kinds of martial arts and honing his mind into the sharpest detective tool ever to grace the pages of any comic book. The laser focus Bruce Wayne employs to achieve his goals is simply legendary. He focuses on anything that makes him advance and neglects everything else. In one comic (*Batman* #0, October 1994), recalling his early years in high school, Batman is described by his school principal as follows: "Genius level in certain subjects, yet almost no retention in others, as if he's focused only on what interests him—to the exclusion of everything else."

This particular issue also adds enlightening words on Bruce Wayne's training to become the Batman: "Upon completing High School, he elected to leach the world of whatever it could offer his specialized needs . . . logging more air miles than he cares to remember as he audited classes in the great universities of Europe and the Far East, absorbing much, but never completing a single course. He studied the disciplines of the body as well, training with enlightened teachers of the martial arts, and mastering many of them. Finally, he sought out the world's finest detectives, and was surprised by the discrepancies between textbook technique and actual fieldwork."

Obsessive, almost insane, focus and discipline are what make Batman so great. Being independently wealthy is a major factor that also contributes to his success (obviously). He doesn't have to worry about making a living to pay the bills—unlike many of us. So all the hours we spend at work are his to use. Of the forty-plus hours a normal person spends on their job, he makes every minute count towards his goal, and then some. Bruce Wayne extended his work hours deep into the night, often skipping sleep altogether just to reach whatever goal he set himself on. Perhaps what sets him apart even further is the fact that Batman possesses no super-powers. He has trained himself physically and mentally to peak human capabilities, but he is still just a man.

I must confess. As a kid growing up, I was very much a Superman fan in every way. When I reached adulthood, though, Batman became more and more appealing to me. I don't think I'm alone in this respect. Most grown men will admit to this. Childhood is when you idolize Superman; adulthood is when you realize Batman makes more sense. Basically, I suppose we identify with Batman for the following reasons:

1. He's human (no superpowers).

2. He's got all the money we wish we had (be honest now).

3. He's good looking and popular with the ladies.

4. He's über smart.

5. He has a good heart (deep down, although it is broken).

6. He's got all the cool gadgets and the toys. Ohhh, the toys!

7. He makes being a superhero appear attainable.

Bottom line: Batman (Bruce Wayne) is everything we wish we could be. And that's just the thing, isn't it? With his billions of dollars, turning himself into a super-effective vigilante could be an actual, although quite remote, possibility—whereas flying in the air and deflecting bullets can never happen. That is why the Dark Knights appeals to a more grown-up audience. A *Facebook* meme, which I found amusing, read, "There are 492 billionaires on earth, and none of those losers decided to become Batman." Sad, isn't it?

LEADERSHIP STYLE

Batman leads from the back . . . very closely from the back. I know it sounds unorthodox or unfit for a leader, but he does it better than anyone, and here is why.

First off, it is not that he is a coward or that he doesn't want to get his hands dirty. You can eliminate that opinion right from the start. You have to understand his circumstances and who he leads. With the exception of his work with Robin, Nightwing, or Batgirl, Batman is often charging into battle with the Justice League, an assemblage of heroes with superpowers galore. Most of them can lift more than sixty tons and/or move at super speed. Why would he take the same risks as them? Besides, his true usefulness for the team lies in his unsurpassed analytical and tactical ability. He could better serve the team by taking a step back to assess the situations they find themselves in. They rely on him for that purpose, and he knows it. While he's not the only leader on the team (sharing this responsibility with Superman and Wonder Woman), he is the one whose advice they lean on more heavily. Is it because he talks in a deep voice? While this helps, it's mostly because they trust his judgement, which rarely fails.

In the same manner, the Batman leader leads his team using his superior knowledge, training, and deep analytical prowess. He's not flashy or in your face, but everybody listens to him. Why? Because he's highly intelligent, authoritative, and rarely wrong. He also has much more experience than the average leader. His track record alone commands respect. The Batman leader cares deeply about his team, but rarely shows it. The Batman leader isn't usually popular and doesn't aim to be. One thing's for sure, though: he's got their back and they know it.

The Batman leader is all about his business, which can make him seem aloof. He is not actually unfriendly; he is just focused. He is task oriented, not people oriented. Sometimes, when the need arises, he will lead from the front in a more take-charge role—especially if he's working with a very inexperienced team (think Batman and Robin). When he does so, you can barely recognize him. He can be very comfortable in assuming that role when there is a need for it, and he does it as well as anyone. It's just not quite his preferred method. Regardless, he is as adaptable as he is competent.

Coming up with a solid game plan is what the Batman leader does best. And if that plan should fail, he is a master at improvising his way out of a slump because, chances are, he pre-calculated the risk of what might go wrong and had a back-up plan all along.

An amusing example of a Batman leader is seen in the persona of Don Draper in the hit TV series *Madmen*. Although quite flawed, he is nevertheless a perfect example of a Batman leader in action in the corporate world. Think about that the next time you watch *Madmen* on Netflix. And, no, I am not getting any royalties for this plug.

STRENGTHS

If there is a problem in your company, community, church, or organization, the Batman leader will most likely be the one to identify it quickly and bring up a solution or strategy to address it. The mind of the Batman leader is his greatest asset. His ability to break up and analyze a problem or situation is uncanny. Also, when he sets a goal, nothing will detract him from attaining it. He is focused, determined, and highly disciplined. He will keep going when all others are ready to cash in their chips. He is highly realistic in his outlook.

Some will call him negative, but that's just not true. If he were negative, he would not be determined. He's just too darn accurate and almost never wrong in his predictions. As a result, when his outlook is more pessimistic, people tend to see him as being negative. No. Chances are, he's just right on—nothing more, nothing less. So if a Batman-type leader comments on one of your projects by saying that it's not going to work, do not misconstrue his criticism as him raining on your parade. He's not being negative or seeing the glass as half-empty; he's simply telling you to find a plan B. These guys are right 99 percent of the time. And the best part is, they learn from their mistakes, which means they are still improving on their 99 percent success rate. It's quite impressive, really, to see a Batman leader putting his mind to work.

Oh, and by the way, if you disagree with them, proving them wrong is a thrill and a half! Just ask Batgirl . . . and Robin . . . and Nightwing . . . and Superman . . . and the Flash . . . and . . .

WEAKNESSES

In the DC animated movie, *Crisis on Two Earths*, the heroes of the Justice League travel to an alternate earth on which their counterparts are evil. In the chilling conclusion, Batman insists on being teleported to an alternate "Earth Prime," which his evil counterpart, Owlman, is seeking to obliterate using a gigantic nuke. Owlman's plot is simple: destroy Earth Prime (the first ever earth from which all other alternate realities stem), and all of the other earths will be obliterated. His megalomaniacal mind perceives this to be the only way to truly make a lasting impact, to matter. Yeah, a real nut job.

Anyway, Batman could have voted Superman (invulnerable and much stronger than the villain) to be teleported to stop Owlman, but instead, he insisted on being the one to go, even though he had a couple of broken ribs from a previous fight earlier in the movie. Bruce Wayne's decision had the fate of all creation in the balance . . . and he didn't send Superman! Why? Owlman said it best when, having the upper hand in the ensuing fight, he told Batman: "You should have sent your flying man. With his strength, he might have had a chance. But you don't trust anyone else to do what needs to be done. I feel the same way." There it is, the main weakness of Batman leaders. They are so intelligent, knowledgeable, and competent that they do not trust others to do as good a job as they would under most circumstances. This can definitely put them at odds with other members of their team.

EFFICIENCY RATING

The Batman leader's efficiency is what sets him apart. While his methods might not always be popular, his results speak for themselves. Pragmatism is the key for this type of leader. He is all about end results. Granted, this might ruffle a few feathers along the way. Most of the time, he doesn't mind. He knows that, in the end, he will still get the accolades of his team. He just knows it.

PEOPLE SKILLS: 6

SMARTS: 10

VISION: 10

CHARACTER: 8

ADAPTABILITY: 10

FOCUS: 10

"IT" FACTOR: 7

OVERALL: 9

CALL TO ACTION: BE DISCIPLINED

"Discipline is remembering what you want."

—DAVID CAMPBELL

If there's one thing we can learn from Batman, it's that you can reach for perfection in your training, your knowledge, and your know-how. Discipline and methodical time management will get you very, very far. We can always improve on what we know and how we do things—on who we are.

If you're going to lead like a superhero, constant self-improvement is crucial. We know that perfection is unattainable, but that doesn't mean we shouldn't aim for it—just like the Batman.

Batman is disciplined because he remembers what he wants—everyday. He wants to honor his parents' memory by making sure criminals are stopped; and he wants to instill fear in them as he does it.

Batman trained himself to peak physical and mental conditioning. Let me repeat that: *Batman trained himself.* Remember, the Dark Knight has no superpowers. He went to all the schools, followed all the courses, underwent all the physical punishment, took all the trips around the world, did all the push-ups, suffered all the sleepless nights, got all the bruises, ate all the right foods, implemented all the schedules and workouts, paid all the experts, ordered all the materials, commissioned the construction of all his gadgets and vehicles, read all the books, sought all the mentors, worked all the hours, calculated all the probabilities, covered all the bases, and took all the precautions to make himself into the most feared and admired superhero on the planet.

His "why" made him into a completely obsessed individual. But you know what? There is no greatness without obsession. In order to achieve greatness, we need to be disciplined, obsessed with excellence, and willing to work our butts off. UFC champion Conor McGregor said, "I am not talented; I am obsessed." This rings true with all those who achieved massive success in history. How obsessed did Thomas Edison have to be to actually try ten thousand times before succeeding with the light bulb? Most of us would have quit after ten failed attempts, let alone ten thousand!

Only obsessed men and women change history. Read about the men and women who have their names in our history books. They were all obsessed with what they were trying to accomplish! So, you want to be great? You want to be like Batman? You want a sharp mind, a fit body, and strong character? Get obsessed with it.

> "There is no greatness without obsession. In order to achieve greatness, we need to be disciplined, obsessed with excellence, and willing to work our butts off."

When I was in high school in Montreal, I was lucky enough be pals with Yanick Paquette. Today, Yanick Paquette is one of the premier comic book artists at DC Comics. At the time of this writing, he just finished a Wonder Woman book with Grant Morrison

(*Wonder Woman: Earth One*, Volume 1). Just so you know, you have to be really good to work with Grant Morrison. He is one of the premier writers in the industry and isn't matched with just any artist.

I got to witness Yanick as a young, sixteen-year-old aspiring comic book artist. He would go to all of his classes with a huge sketching pad and pencils. While he listened to the teacher, he was always doodling something, owning his already impressive skill. In the classrooms, at the cafeteria, outside on the campus, he was always drawing. As a result, his skill grew exponentially into what it is today. It was a privilege to witness his talent every day, even though, I have to admit, I was a bit jealous at the time—and too short sighted to ask for a few autographed drawings (ugh!). The point is this: he went from good to excellent by relentlessly beating on his craft every day. He was disciplined; he was obsessed. Excellence in any endeavor, including leadership, can only be achieved by aiming for it through rigid discipline.

I've heard many times from many different people that "only the elite can reach the top." That's just not true. It's the other way around: they are the elite because they have reached the top. People don't realize the effort and relentlessness most successful leaders have put in to get where they are.

So, how about you? Is there any aspect of your life that needs work? Are you not in good physical condition? Work out. Be intentional and make a workable plan to get in shape. Thirty minutes a day is great, but you can also do twenty minutes three times a week—whatever works for you. Are your relationships lacking? Are you alienated from your spouse, your parents, or your children? Read a good book on relationships or seek out good advice or counseling. Is there an area in your field of expertise that you need to acquire more knowledge in?

Go to seminars, follow a course, or read books that will correct that. Jim Rohn, who was a business philosopher, said, "Work harder on yourself than you do at your job."

Most of us want to be Batman, but very few of us are actually willing to do what he did to achieve it. It's really up to you. So, tell me, how many push-ups did you do today?

WHAT OTHERS HAD TO SAY

"It took them a while to catch on that Batman would be the greatest."

—BOB KANE, CREATOR OF BATMAN

"I don't think he likes me very much."

—THE FLASH

"I don't think he likes anyone very much."

—MARTIAN MANHUNTER

"We all wake up in the morning, wanting to live our lives the way we know we should. But we usually don't, in small ways. That's what makes a character like Batman so fascinating. He plays out our conflicts on a much larger scale."

—CHRISTOPHER NOLAN, DIRECTOR OF *BATMAN BEGINS*

"You could try asking people nicely."

—SUPERMAN, TO BATMAN

"I used to think I actually was Batman."

—JUSTIN TIMBERLAKE, SINGER/ACTOR

"Batman has been acknowledged as a legend in my lifetime."

—BOB KANE, CREATOR OF BATMAN

CHAPTER 6

THE CAPTAIN AMERICA

THE BRILLIANT UNIFIER AND STRATEGIST

"Why someone weak? Because a weak man knows the value of strength, the value of power."

—CAPTAIN AMERICA

CHARACTER BIO

Stemming from the collective imagination of Joe Simon and Jack Kirby, the Captain America character first appeared in *Captain America Comics* #1 (cover dated March 1941). The flag-and-shield-wielding superhero is the alter ego of Steve Rogers. The origin of Captain America is born of wartime when his creators felt America needed a new superhero who would fight the Germans and uplift the morale of the troops and the population. It's also a real underdog-to-glory fairy tale. You see, Steve Rogers was too frail to enlist in the army. But his repeated efforts, bravery, and resilience caught the attention of the upper echelons of the military. Through a secret project called Project: Rebirth, they offered him to become a test subject to a serum they had created. If successful, the experiment would make Rogers into a super-soldier. It was successful. A leader was born, um, er, made. Geez . . . which is it?!

After fighting for America in World War II, Captain America's plane is shot down, and the hero falls into the frozen North Atlantic Ocean. Obviously, he is believed dead—that is, until they recover his frozen body decades later! After successfully being unfrozen and brought back to life, Captain America just picked up the fight where he left off. He is still fighting the good fight as we speak.

Regardless of what your political views are, you cannot dislike Captain America. Why? Because Cap stands for the things that unite all Americans, not for any issue that divides them. He is the comic book version of a founding father and the ultimate unifier.

As a result of the super-soldier serum, Captain America is a nearly perfect human being with peak human strength, agility, stamina, and intelligence. But what's even greater about him is that he retained his good moral values, compassion, and integrity. Those powers Steve Rogers gained through the super-soldier serum injection would be nothing if they were not wielded by this fine example of a man. It's Captain America's heart and mind that sets him apart; it's his character. Oh, and his shield . . . his amazing, unbreakable, vibranium alloy shield and the way he throws it around like a boomerang—yeah, that too.

LEADERSHIP STYLE

Superman is more powerful; Batman is cooler; Spider-Man is more amazing; Wolverine is more badass. But ask anyone in the know to link the word leadership with any superhero and chances are, Captain America will come out on top. Remember, this is not a book about who the best superhero is. It's a book about leadership. And Cap is all about leadership—heck, that's his superpower! He is even the ultimate leader as far as superheroes are concerned. I'm not just saying this; I have proof.

When Marvel and DC did the JLA/Avengers crossover in 2003, the heroes of both universes are seen battling it out for at least half the book—until they come to their senses and decide to join forces in order to defeat their cosmic foe: Krona. A turning point in the book comes when Superman says, "We need a commander—someone who can lead both teams, fuse us into one." He then turns to Cap and adds, "I believe that should be you, Captain America."

The Captain then says, with his trademark humility, "I'm flattered, but I'm not so sure. The conflicting nature of our two worlds has put us on edge . . . frayed tempers . . . judgments . . .

"I know, but you're still the man for the job."

And the icing on the cake comes when Batman says, "I concur."

Talk about being voted MVP by your peers! Batman and Superman both see him as the best leader for this "end of the world as we know it" scenario, not to mention the rest of those two hall of fame teams, the JLA and Avengers! That's how strong the leadership ability of this comic book icon is.

There is a saying, "If you don't stand for something, you will fall for anything." Captain America stands for something: America's values and ideals (the vintage ones). And because he stands so strongly for those, he rarely, if ever, falls for anything else.

Don't be fooled like I was. I used to think that Captain America was a bit naïve politically. I thought he was easily manipulated into doing what the government wanted him to do. I was very wrong. Steve Engleheart, who wrote Captain America during the Vietnam War, had this to say: "He stands for America as an ideal, not America as it's practiced."

This distinction is crucial to understand the Captain's character. He stands for the timeless values that once made America great: freedom, liberty, justice, and doing what's right—no matter the cost.

Captain America's strength of character was made even more evident in the Marvel series titled *Civil War*. In it, Captain America takes a stand against government policies that state superheroes should disclose their secret identities to the public. Here is what he says:

> Doesn't matter what the press says. Doesn't matter what the politicians or the mobs say. Doesn't matter if the whole country decides that something wrong is something right. This nation was founded on one principle above all else: the requirement that we stand up for what we believe, no matter the odds or the consequences. When the mob and the press and the whole world tell you to move, your job is to plant yourself like a tree beside the river of truth and to tell the whole world, "No, you move." (*Amazing Spider-Man* #537, December 2006).

Is there such a thing as a perfect leader? Is there a way of leading that would be the perfect combination of courage, savvy, wisdom, vision, people skills, and sheer determination? While there may not be any perfect leaders out there, one could argue that in the comics, Captain America is as close to perfection as they come. Captain America leaders get their hands dirty. They are right there alongside their staff, in the trenches, shoulder to shoulder. And if you have the privilege of working with a leader like that, you should thank your lucky stars and try to learn as much from him as you possibly can. If you are a leader who exhibits many of these qualities, keep it up. You're doing great!

My favorite book says that not acting in accordance with your convictions is a sin. Well, in that respect, I guess Cap leaders are pretty much saints because they always act out of conviction. Even if that conviction is the fruit of much thought and deliberation, in the end, they always stand firm. Unimpeachable character and integrity defines them.

Captain America leaders don't lead from the comfort of a leather chair, podium, or office. They do as much as they say because they love to be in the heart of the action. They love the thrill that a new challenge brings, and they rise to the occasion again and again. They hate sitting on the sidelines. They lead their team, but they are also part of their team—and everybody knows it. They reassure, empower, inspire, and enable others to be the best they can be. They are followed because they are fully trusted. They earn that trust through their actions.

There is a scene in *The Avengers* movie (2012) that I absolutely love. In it, the Chitauri (aliens) are wreaking havoc in NYC and spreading pandemonium. After running through a barrage of obstacles and laser fire, Cap lands on top of a car in the middle of a group of cops, who are obviously and understandably overwhelmed by the situation. He addresses the sergeant, and the ensuing conversation goes like this:

> **CAPTAIN AMERICA:** You need men in these buildings. There are people inside, and they're going to be running right into the line of fire. You take them to the basements or through the subway. You keep them off the streets. I need a perimeter as far back as 39th.

> **POLICE SERGEANT:** Why the hell should I take orders from you?

> [The Chitauri attack. Cap blocks a blast with his shield, bats one Chitauri away with it, then blocks a point-blank assault, and punches another in the face. He grabs one of their weapons and then punches the Chitauri, flinging it across the street.]

> **POLICE SERGEANT (TO HIS STAFF):** I need men in those buildings. Lead the people down and away from the streets. We're going to set up a perimeter all the way down 39th Street.

Yep, actions definitely speak louder than words. That's how Captain America leaders lead: in the thick of the action and by taking massive action. Who they are speaks so loud that they do not need to repeat what they say. They make themselves heard through action.

STRENGTHS

Cap leaders are firmly intentional. They leave nothing to chance, and there is always a reason behind everything they say or do, even if sometimes these might not be apparent. If you question them, their answer makes you realize that they are at least two steps ahead of everybody—ahead of you. They have already concocted contingency plans: B in case A fails and a C and a D plan as well. They're never short on strategy. They've covered every base, and you're covered as well.

Cap leaders are task oriented and people oriented. This sets them apart in a huge way. Most leaders are one or the other. Cap leaders are both—and great at both! They tend to make all members on their team more efficient. They are extremely gifted in assessing the strengths and liabilities of their team. They will make sure your strengths are exploited and that others can work around your weaknesses.

Cap leaders are the epitome of self-sacrifice. In the end, they'll always take the blame for any failure on the team. They are humble and will never ask you to do anything they're not willing to do themselves. They usually come from humble beginnings and have earned their stripes. Their empathy and wisdom also earn them the respect of their team.

WEAKNESSES

Captain America leaders have impeccable strength of character. On the other hand, these types of leaders tend to be more "old school." Their high moral stance can sometimes put them at odds with, shall we say, team members who are a bit more laid back, progressive, freethinking, or simply less engaged. They can be overly serious at times, and "fun" is not a big part of their vocabulary. Cap leaders have little tolerance for those who put in half-assed efforts, and this may sometimes lead to conflicting views.

EFFICIENCY RATING

The overall leadership efficiency of Captain America leaders is the gold standard. Leadership is influence, and Cap leaders are all about that. They lead by word and deed, and those under them know that they say what they mean and mean what they say. Usually, the followers of Cap leaders will follow them to hell and back. They inspire trust and energize their team with passion.

In the JLA/Avengers crossover, when the two teams are fighting innumerable enemies alongside one another, they are telepathically linked together by the Martian Manhunter. That way, they can "hear" Captain America's directions directly in their minds. At one point, Cap is giving out orders left and right, efficiently leading them into battle without hesitation. The Atom, turning to Vision, says, "I'll say this; the man knows what he wants. He always this impressive, Vision?" And Vision answers, "Always."

The Captain America leader is just like that, always impressive. As John Maxwell, author of *The 21 Irrefutable Laws of Leadership*, put it, "A leader is one who knows the way, goes the way, and shows the way." That sums it up right there. That is the essence of what these types of leaders are and do—and then some. Imagine all of the qualities of a great leader embodied in one person: courage, character, integrity, vision, authority, strength, intelligence, and, last but not least, the capacity to unite a team into one cohesive group. This is what the Captain America-type leader epitomizes.

Of course, I am fully aware of the rarity of such a brand of leadership. One could even say that it is utopic to think that such leaders exist in the first place. Some would say that this is the stuff of fiction. I'm not going to argue. Perfection is not of this world—even Cap falls short on rare occasions. However, shouldn't perfection be our aim? If a leader wants to emulate Captain America in his leadership style, it is a very noble and worthy endeavor. I believe it is even a method that should be taught in business schools and in leadership training. I am not kidding. Many valuable leadership lessons could be gained from a thorough study of Captain America in the comics.

PEOPLE SKILLS: 9

SMARTS: 10

VISION: 10

CHARACTER: 10

ADAPTABILITY: 10

FOCUS: 10

"IT" FACTOR: 10

OVERALL: 10

CALL TO ACTION: DEVELOP A STRONG CHARACTER

Captain America is a model of strong character. He always does the right thing, no matter what. While it's true that the super-soldier serum gave him exceptional ability, let's not forget why he was chosen for that experiment in the first place: he was relentless, obsessed with excellence, self-sacrificing, and showed remarkable integrity. He wanted to be enlisted and stopped at nothing to get there—all this in spite of a frail body and poor genetics.

When choosing players for the NFL, MLB, NBA, or NHL, character joins speed, size, and skill as a necessary trait. As teams prepare for the draft, players with questionable character fall in priority. Most of the time when teams choose high-risk players, the down side outweighs any benefit from their ability. Pro sports isn't the only place where character counts. It counts in every walk of life. Do you pay enough attention to character building in your life?

Having a strong character means doing the right thing just because it is the right thing to do—even when nobody is watching.

But what is strong character made of? Basically, it is made of all the good and noble qualities found in the heart of man. Our character is much more than just our reputation or personality. It is who we are, even when no one is watching. Having a strong character means doing the right thing just because it is the right thing to do—even when nobody is watching. Fairly simple, isn't it?

Norman Schwarzkopf, the famous Desert Storm general, once said, "Most leadership failures that occur don't happen for lack of competence, but for lack of character." Ain't that the truth!

So how does one build up good and upstanding character? Well, just model Captain America. Not enough? Okay, I'll give you more to chew on. Here are a few sure ways to improve in your character.

- ★ Model and emulate great people from history.
- ★ Pursue virtue, wisdom, and understanding.
- ★ Seek out good company.
- ★ Build people up through your words and actions.
- ★ Mind your tongue.

★ Keep your emotions in check.

★ Always act out of conviction.

★ Have integrity.

★ Be a person of your word.

★ Ask those around you, whom you trust, to tell you about your weaknesses, and try to improve in those areas.

Strong character can only be found in people who have high moral standards. Captain America has very high moral standards. Of course, building strong character like that exemplified by Cap is not done in a day. Building character isn't microwaveable. It's a process—more like a crock-pot recipe. It takes time, and you need to be patient with yourself. Be firm and intentional about it, and you could become a fantastic leader. It's what the Captain would do.

WHAT OTHERS HAD TO SAY

"This is why you were chosen. Because the strong man, who has known power all his life, may lose respect for that power, but a weak man knows the value of strength and knows . . . compassion."

—DR. ABRAHAM ERSKINE, CREATOR OF THE SUPER-SOLDIER SERUM IN THE COMICS

"When Captain America is in a room full of Marvel superheroes, he is always Top Dog, even though his powers are pretty modest. He could be stood next to Thor, Iron Man, whomever. He is the one that everyone looks up to."

—GARY FRANK, PENCILER FOR DC AND MARVEL

"I always wanted to see why Captain America was on this team of Avengers. He's got to have a reason—he can't just be really fast and punch really hard."

—CHRIS EVANS, ACTOR

"I decided to make Captain America *because I realized I wasn't doing the film because it terrified me. You can't make decisions based on fear."*

—CHRIS EVANS, ACTOR

CHAPTER 7

THE WONDER WOMAN

THE STRONG AND VERSATILE FEMALE LEAD

★　　★　　★　　★　　★

"Don't kill if you can wound; don't wound if you can subdue; don't subdue if you can pacify; and don't raise your hand at all until you've first extended it."

—WONDER WOMAN

CHARACTER BIO

Wise as Athena, stronger than Hercules, swift as Hermes, and beautiful as Aphrodite: this is the description of the most powerful and influential female superhero in comics. Wonder Woman (Princess Diana) first appeared in *Sensation Comics* #1 (January 1942) and was created by Charles Moulton and H. G. Peter. She is the ultimate female superhero and, like Superman, has set the standard for all the others.

As the story goes, she was miraculously conceived from clay by the gods in answer to the prayers of her mother, Queen Hippolyta of the Amazons (from Greek mythology). Each of the following six deities also granted Diana a gift: Demeter, great strength; Athena, wisdom and courage; Artemis, a hunter's heart and a communion with animals; Aphrodite, beauty and a loving heart; Hestia, sisterhood with fire; Hermes, speed and the power of flight. Diana grew up surrounded by a legion of sisters and mothers, most of them warriors in their own right.

When she was a young woman, the gods decreed that the Amazons must send an emissary into Man's World. Queen Hippolyta ordered a contest to be held, but forbade Diana from participating. Diana disobeyed and participated in disguise, easily winning the contest and being named the Amazons' champion. She was given a uniform fashioned from the standard of someone (an American) who had visited the island a few decades earlier. She was also given a lasso of truth, which was forged by the god Hephaestus from the Golden Girdle of Gaea. The lasso is completely unbreakable, immutable, and indestructible. It compels anyone bound by it to speak truthfully. She also wears unbreakable bracelets forged from the shield of Zeus, which can deflect projectiles, and a razor sharp tiara, which can be used as a boomerang-type weapon. In more recent times, she also carries an unbreakable sword, forged by Hephaestus himself. When declared the Amazons' champion, Diana was dispatched as an emissary and sent off to America. This is where she's been fighting the good fight ever since as one of the world's best-known superheroes.

Few people know that among her arsenal of phenomenal powers, Diana also has supernatural empathy and charisma, which was granted by Athena (Goddess of Wisdom). The "Sight of Athena," as it is called, apparently grants her increased insight. For example, Diana can often detect others' emotions. Oh, and she can also communicate with animals.

LEADERSHIP STYLE

Most people think of Wonder Woman as a female version of Superman. Although their power levels are similar, many things set them apart. Superman possesses many superpowers, but they can be scientifically explained. Wonder Woman's powers, on the other hand, are supernatural. For example, she possesses the skills of a master tactician and strategist, granted by Athena (Goddess of Wisdom). As a result, Diana is accomplished in the arts of leadership, persuasion, and diplomacy; she possesses great courage as well. She is a highly gifted, *supernatural* leader. Also, her supernatural empathy gives her incredible people skills. Superman had to foster those skills. Here is what Diana, the diplomat, once said in the comics:

> If the prospect of living in a world where trying to respect the basic rights of those around you and valuing each other simply because we exist are such daunting, impossible tasks that only a superhero born of royalty can address them, then what sort of world are we left with? And what sort of world do you want to live in? (*Wonder Woman* #170)

The wisdom displayed in this quote exemplifies the essence of Wonder Woman. But aside from her remarkable wisdom and insight, Diana is all warrior. Surprised? Batman once said that "Wonder Woman is the best melee fighter in the world." And, interestingly, the Big Three of DC Comics once had the following conversation:

WONDER WOMAN (WW): Come on, Kal, I am faster than you.

SUPERMAN: How can you possibly believe that?

WW: Because I've sparred with you.

SUPERMAN: Excuse me, Diana. Super-speed?

WW: Certainly you have an advantage in raw speed, but you have to think before you respond. I'm a trained warrior; my reactions are in my muscle memory.

SUPERMAN (TURNING TO BATMAN): What do you say, Bruce? Break the tie.

BATMAN: I don't think you'll like my answer.

SUPERMAN: Oh, not you too?

BATMAN: Who's faster, Usain Bolt or Bruce Lee?

Indeed, when it comes to making quick decisions, whether physical or mental, Wonder Woman has no equal. This is especially true when she needs to act as a leader, diplomat, or negotiator. Her knowledge of how to relate to people is what makes her stand out. Someone once said that women are the relational experts of the human race. I agree. My wife also reminds me every day. She communicates a great deal more than I do. Emotional connectivity and depth usually enables women to connect better with people than most men can.

Making people get along and go along is the modus operandi of the Wonder Woman leader. She thrives in group dynamics where complex and often differing personalities need to mesh together towards a common goal. She can take a tense and divergent environment and make it peaceable and harmonious, with only a short pep talk or swift decision. She is a master at making tough calls and tough decisions. The Wonder Woman leader is the best melee diplomat and peacemaker in the world. By the way, Batman didn't say this. I did.

The American Psychological Association published a study in 2003 (APA [2003] *Psychological Bulletin* Vol. 129, No. 4, 569–591) entitled, *Transformational, Transactional, and Laissez-Faire Leadership Styles: A Meta-Analysis Comparing Women and Men.* The following analysis is given:

> The possibility that women and men differ in their typical leadership behavior is important because leaders' own behavior is a major determinant of their effectiveness and chances for advancement. In this article, we focus on leadership style, which we define as relatively stable patterns of behavior displayed by leaders. Claims about the distinctive leadership styles of women abound, especially in treatments by writers of trade books (e.g., Book, 2000; Helgesen, 1990; Loden, 1985; Rosener, 1995). In analyzes that draw on personal experience in organizations and on informal surveys and interviews of managers, these writers have maintained that female leaders, compared with male leaders, are less hierarchical, more cooperative and collaborative, and more oriented to enhancing others' self-worth. Moreover, such authors have also argued that these patterns of behavior make women superior leaders for contemporary organizations. This theme of female excellence in leadership has been echoed by journalists—for example, in *BusinessWeek's* special report that appeared under the headline, "As leaders, women rule: New studies find that female managers outshine their male counterparts in almost

every measure" (Sharpe, 2000) and in *Fast Company's* article on female CEOs, which declared that "the future of business depends on women" (Hefferman, 2002, p. 9).

As the face of corporate leadership has transformed over the years, so have the methods that comprise it. And in our contemporary, people-focused, and customer-service-driven economy, women's relational skills are putting them in a class of their own. By saying this, I am by no means saying that women are better leaders than men. All I am saying is that their unique predispositions may give them an advantage in today's corporate needs in leadership.

Enter the Wonder Woman-type leader. You've probably met one. They excel at their jobs (and at home). Their groomed personal appearance is top notch. They know exactly what they want and how to get it. They have integrity, decisiveness, and a warrior spirit. They are skilled at what they do and have people skills to boot. They are confident, but not arrogant. They say what they mean and they mean what they say—but are never mean. Such qualities, if they emanated from a man, would be greatly admired and revered. Unfortunately for the Wonder Woman leaders of this world, though, they sometimes end up with negative reviews and have to work harder just to earn the respect they deserve. This by no means diminishes their worth. And this worth is just going to be trending upward with the new business models and leadership needs for today. Wonder Woman leaders are masters of EQ.

STRENGTHS

The strengths of the Wonder Woman leader are very similar to the ones found among the best of her male counterparts. She is smart, driven, focused, and excels at people skills. Her driven nature belies her innate compassion and care for those under her. A good Wonder Woman leader will not only prove her worth by her accomplishments, but will also gain the respect of even the most reticent among her peers. She is not only determined but highly charismatic and, well, kind.

Consider the movie *What Women Want*, starring Mel Gibson and Helen Hunt. The character played by Hunt was the prototypical Wonder Woman leader in action. She is skilled, smart, and good with people. But she also has a strong emotional nature. At the end of the movie, we know how good she is and that she deserves to be in the driver's seat at her job.

WEAKNESSES

If she tries to emulate her male counterparts by acting and leading like they do, she loses what sets her apart. She rarely, if ever, falls for that because she generally has very high confidence in herself. Nevertheless, at times of self-doubt, she might resort to this out of emotional vulnerability, which only undermines her overall efficiency. She may also resist men's advice because of pride. The fact that she grew up on an island inhabited by only women might explain it. Fortunately, this isn't often the case for the real Wonder Woman leaders out there.

EFFICIENCY RATING

Gifted across the board; Wonder Woman leaders are a force to be reckoned with in organizations or communities where they serve. They are confident, proud, and highly efficient. They are also highly valued for their energetic contributions, communication skills, and swift decisive abilities in times of unrest.

PEOPLE SKILLS: 10

SMARTS: 9

VISION: 9

CHARACTER: 10

ADAPTABILITY: 10

FOCUS: 9

"IT" FACTOR: 10

OVERALL: 9

CALL TO ACTION: BE DECISIVE

He told her that only death would stop him. So, she held his head in her hands and looked at him as their eyes locked; then, swiftly and effortlessly . . . CRAAACK! His neck broken, Maxwell Lord, the shrewd and powerful businessman, fell to the ground; his limp body, now lifeless, lay at the feet of Diana. The tragic execution went viral in the media all over the world. The peace-making Wonder Woman was now seen as a ruthless executioner—not only by the people, but also by her Justice League peers, especially Superman and Batman. The subsequent ripples of that decision by the Amazon brought about the disbandment of The Justice League. It was a tough decision, made by a tough and decisive heroine, but the price to pay was very high for Wonder Woman. I mean, superheroes (especially those of the DC universe) aren't supposed to kill, right?

We all know what desperate times call for, but what was the motive of her decision? What pushed her to such desperate measures? First off, Maxwell Lord was a very bad man. Period. Perhaps you think that alone doesn't justify resorting to taking lethal action.

I agree. But there's more. Secondly, he was mind-controlling Superman to do his evil bidding, which could have resulted in the death of countless innocent individuals, including Batman. Thirdly, he told Wonder Woman, in no uncertain terms, that only death would stop him. Now, I ask you: what would you have done?

Sometimes life pushes us to a fork in the road where we need to choose to act as a hero or as a warrior. Wonder Woman chose the warrior's way in this instance.

I have a saying that I like to use, and it goes like this: "Don't complain about your life being tough if you're not willing to make tough decisions." True leadership entails the responsibility of making hard decisions. How you make those tough decisions will determine how others will perceive you as a leader. You might end up being loved, or hated, but one thing is for sure: you will leave no one indifferent. Theodore Roosevelt had this to say about tough decisions: "In any moment of decision, the best thing to do is the right thing, the second best thing to do is the wrong thing, and the worse thing to do is nothing."

> ### "Don't complain about your life being tough if you're not willing to make tough decisions."

If there is one thing Wonder Woman is, it's this: she's decisive. She fully understands that he who hesitates is lost. And she also practices this simple principle: strive for peace; prepare for war. Of all the comic book leaders in this book, I believe Wonder Woman is the best example of this seemingly contradictory principle. She's all about peace, but don't get on her bad side. She understands you can get a lot farther with a kind word and a sword, than with a kind word alone. This duality in her character is perhaps hard to grasp, but it is, nevertheless, what brings her leadership to the highest level. Wonder Woman's capacity to be always kind, yet to make those tough, even ruthless, decisions, makes her an incredibly gifted leader. Even Superman and Batman struggle with this at times. Case in point: how many thousands of people have the Joker and Lex Luthor killed over the years because their necks were never broken? I will not embark on an ethics debate here, but you get my point.

Years ago, the pastor at my local church believed I had some potential and decided to use church funds to send me to a leadership retreat and seminar for a weekend. When I arrived, I had to register, and the man jotting down my info asked me if I wanted a button or a sticker for my nametag. As I hesitated between the two, he laughingly told me, "Young man, if you're going to be a leader, you're going to have to be more decisive than that, especially with the simple stuff." Although he ruffled my feathers a bit at the time, that remark stuck with me to this day. I have since made it a point to be more decisive.

Ever since women have entered the corporate leadership world, they have had to fight, generally twice as hard as men, to earn leadership positions and the respect that comes with it. It's been an uphill climb, but many Wonder Women out there have proven just as capable as their male counterparts and have proven, quite impressively, the old adage that says, "It's not the size of the dog in the fight, but the size of the fight in the dog that counts." It's what's in you that counts. The ability to make tough decisions stems from what's in you, your self-confidence, and from the ability to keep your gaze forward. So, how good are you at making those tough decisions? Do you have it in you? If not, it may be time to toughen up.

WHAT OTHERS HAD TO SAY

"Ultimately, she's about truth, and it's all heart with her. She's a strong female force . . . She's strong, but she's so much more—not everybody gets that."

—LINDA CARTER, ACTRESS

"If you need to stop an asteroid, you call Superman. If you need to solve a mystery, you call Batman. But if you need to end a war, you call Wonder Woman."

—GAIL SIMONE, WRITER

"In our community, we simplify Superman and Batman into the light and the dark sides of our nature. Wonder Woman encompasses both. Completely maternal and caring, and all the best qualities a person could have . . . but I've seen her at war with an axe in her hand. And that's where the sweetness stops."

—BLACK CANARY

"Wonder Woman isn't Spider-Man or Batman. She doesn't have a town; she has a world. That was more interesting to me than a kind of contained, rote superhero franchise."

—JOSS WHEDON, WRITER

"I feel like Diana is really accessible. It's very easy to relate to her. She has the heart of a human so she can be emotional, she's curious, she's compassionate, she loves people. And then she has the powers of a goddess. She's all for good, she fights for good, she believes in great. I want to be her."

—GAL GADOT, ACTRESS

CHAPTER 8
THE WOLVERINE
THE PASSIONATE
SITUATIONAL LEADER

"In my whole life, I felt like an animal. I ignored my instincts, and I ignored what I really am. And that won't ever happen again."

—WOLVERINE

CHARACTER BIO

"I'm the best there is at what I do, but what I do best isn't very nice." Those aren't the words of your typical hero; those are the words of the fearsome mutant Wolverine.

Born as James Howlett and commonly known as Logan, the Marvel character first appeared in the last panel of *The Incredible Hulk* #180, with his first full appearance in #181 (cover dated November 1974).

Wolverine is a mutant. He possesses animal-keen senses, enhanced physical capabilities, and a powerful regenerative ability known as a "healing factor." Oh, and the claws, let's not forget those three-foot-long claws he has on each hand: Snikt! Although, on a personal note,

I would prefer "Tchink" to "Snikt," but I don't have a say on the matter. Anyway, the claws are an extension of his skeleton, which was reinforced with adamantium, a rare, unbreakable metal. So, with an unbreakable skeleton and a healing factor to boot, Wolverine is practically impossible to kill. He also sports a nasty attitude and likes to drink and smoke cigars. On the outside, he's just the kind of guy you don't want your daughter to bring home. In fact, if you're like me and you have two daughters, you actually pray that they will never bring a guy like this home. No joke.

Known as "Weapon X" to the Canadian government, Wolverine owes his adamantium skeleton to their torturous underground experiments. Yeah, like me, the berserker-raging Logan is a Canuck, and like me, he was created in 1974. The similarities end there. I wish I could say we are kindred spirits, but I'd be lying . . . but I digress.

Ahem . . . so when the underground Canadian government learned about his healing factor, they began experimenting on James Howlett, and through those experiments, he was subjected to the worst kinds of torture. Their aim was to make their own version of Captain America. Well, obviously, that didn't quite go as planned. I suppose that's what happens when the Canadian government tries to emulate their neighbors to the south (tsk, tsk). You see, Logan freed himself and killed all of them in the process. Minor glitch, right? Anyway, after wandering in the Canadian wilderness for a while and surviving by eating game, he was brought back to sanity (and humanity) by the care of a husband and wife team of good Samaritans.

Today, Wolverine fights the good fight—albeit by his own rules. He's been an X-man (X-Force, X boyfriend . . . a lot of X's), an Avenger, and a surprisingly efficient leader when called upon to lead. Logan has suffered much. He's had many of his own inner demons to fight. It could actually be said of him that most of his deadliest enemies are found within. But he's never been known to back down from a fight.

LEADERSHIP STYLE

Wolverine, a leader? I know this may seem a bit far-fetched to some because, first off, Logan is more of an anti-hero than a superhero and, secondly, because he's more of a loner who severely lacks people skills. Yeah, I know all about that. But don't forget that, at his core, James Howlett has more potential than we give him credit for. Think about it.

According to the comics storyline, Wolverine was born in Cold Lake, Alberta, Canada, sometime between 1882 and 1885. This means he's been around the block a few times, which translates into much experience. With his increased lifespan and journeys across the globe, he has been able to amass an intimate knowledge of many foreign customs and cultures. His exploits have enabled him to gather vast knowledge of literature, culture, and philosophy. His brutish nature also hides a very high intelligence. For example, when Wolverine's vitals were monitored during a Danger Room training session, the report stated Logan's physical and mental state was "equivalent to an Olympic-level gymnast performing a gold-medal-winning routine whilst simultaneously beating four chess computers in his head." Impressive, isn't it? Not quite what we would expect from the feral, animalistic Logan.

Wolverine is also fluent in many languages, including English, Arabic, Japanese, Russian, Chinese, Cheyenne, Lakota, and Spanish.

He has some knowledge of French, German, Thai, Vietnamese, Farsi, and Portuguese. Also keep in mind he was initially chosen by his government to be the Canadian Captain America. In fact, he has so much potential that he was first approached by James MacDonald Hudson (aka Guardian, of the Canadian superhero team Alpha Flight) to be the leader of Alpha Flight! And later in his hero career, Cyclops, the distinguished leader of the X-Men, requested that he lead X-Force. So they saw something in him, and that something was, yep, leadership.

I can already hear the fanboys crying at the injustice: "He put Wolverine ahead of Scott Summers (Cyclops), who is the leader of the X-Men!" Actually, guys, this is not a leadership rankings book. It is a leadership *style* analysis. Unfortunately for Mr. Summers, his style is a bit too similar to that of Captain America—but not quite as good—so he got booted. Wolverine, on the other hand, is the perfect prototype of the unlikely leader who rises to the occasion in the darkest moments, the one who comes out of a crisis situation and takes charge, when no one else seems to have the gall. He is the leader who stands up and gets everybody on board through sheer inspiration and passion. Because as far as emotional, passionate, gutsy leadership is concerned, Logan has tons of it. He's what you would call a born leader . . . with none of the refinements.

That's just it, isn't it? Let's face it. Wolverine lacks people skills; he is uncouth and says what he thinks. He is not very nice, but there's something about him. At his core, his heart is good. When he does make up his mind to work alongside you, he shines. He's tireless and won't give up. He's inspiring and motivating to a degree that is rarely found among the classiest men. He's just made of sheer passion, determination, and drive—and he's got your back!

He's willing to self-sacrifice. You wouldn't hire him as a leader if he handed you his CV, but when you see him at work, you get it. I guess that's it with Logan; he's just one of those guys "you have to be there and see him do it" to believe it. It's a case of "you have to be there." Wolverine leaders are different because they generally do not seek to lead; they just take the lead.

In some ways, he's very much like the William Wallace (Braveheart) of superheroes. He's all passion and determination. Burning with intensity and emotional fire, you can't help but want to follow men and women who exhibit such passion and zeal. Their "X" factor is through the roof, and that's how they influence others. For some leaders, it's just about getting it done. It's not about style or grace or reputation or principles—it's about results. Wolverine leaders are like that. If it needs to be done and no one else will do it, they will rise up to meet the challenge. They are often blue collar, courageous, grassroots, organic-type leaders . . . and their fiery passion is contagious.

There is a time and a place for situational leaders like Wolverine. Wolverine leaders are not your typical positional leaders, heads of corporations or organizations who are elected or put in place for a specific purpose. They often rise up in a crisis, most likely at the grassroots level. They often step up when there is no leader around to take care of things. Whenever there is an unmet need for leadership, they pop up to fill the gap.

STRENGTHS

Wolverine leaders' strengths are obvious the moment they are engaged and fully intentional about a project. In fact, once engaged, they are right up there among the best of them! Passionate, intelligent, bold, strong, sacrificial, and fearless are the qualities they espouse best. Their dogged determination to get it done, no matter what, is a trait that everybody admires. They'll complete it alone if they have to. They are quite seasoned and work very well with a younger, more inexperienced team. The reason is simple: when they know for a fact that they're being looked up to, they live up to it. They understand the honor that comes from being trusted by others. Also, their ragged edge and cynicism belies a surprisingly high intelligence. However . . .

WEAKNESSES

Even when they are trying to keep their bluntness, sarcasm, and aggressiveness in check, their people skills or, should I say, lack thereof can be quite detrimental to their effectiveness—and their team. Some of them may even be uncouth.

Often, it may take quite a bit of convincing to get them going on a project. If they don't believe in it, there's just no use. Wolverine leaders run hot . . . or cold. So their lack of engagement can be a problem. They also prefer to work alone—very much so.

EFFICIENCY RATING

Wolverine leaders are rated as the poorest leader-types in this book because of their reluctant engagement and poor people skills. However, the salvation of the Wolverine leaders in our organizations or communities lies in the fact that their quasi-animalistic "IT" Factor gives them the equivalent of a leadership healing factor. People forgive them their faults because the value they add weighs heavier than their shortcomings.

PEOPLE SKILLS: 4

SMARTS: 8

VISION: 7

CHARACTER: 7

ADAPTABILITY: 7

FOCUS: 9

"IT" FACTOR: 10

OVERALL: 7

CALL TO ACTION: BE PASSIONATE

"Passion will move men beyond themselves, beyond their shortcomings, beyond their failures."

—JOSEPH CAMPBELL

Fiery passion always fuels great achievements. It doesn't matter how flawed we are; genuine passion will see us through. Wolverine's achievements are often quite brutal, but they do give his team the victory in the end. Some say Wolverine displays berserker rages; I prefer the term "passionate impulses" or "energy surges." Don't buy it? Okay, so he's flawed, like we all are. In fact, on paper, he seems too flawed to lead effectively. Yet, in spite of this, he rises to the occasion again and again. So if he can do it, why can't we? And don't give me the "I don't have a healing factor or adamantium claws" excuse. That just won't fly here, bub. Lesson learned: no matter what your flaws, you can still bring something valuable to the table if you are passionate and engaged. Passion results in energy. And energy fuels and energizes teams towards their goals. The passion of the leader will determine the energy of his team.

In their book *The Servant Leader*, Ken Blanchard and Phil Hodges write, "No organization will rise above the passion of the leader." Passion is what defines Wolverine—and the Wolverine leader. Hence it is also what makes him a good leader, if perhaps not great. So the object lesson of this call to action is quite simple: How much fire is there in you? Have you found your purpose? Are you passionate? Are your emotions the fuel to your fire, or do you allow them to be a liability to your leadership? What can you do to funnel your emotions into passion?

Erika Andersen, in an article for *Forbes* wrote about the importance of passionate leadership:

> Real passion provides inspiration that's much deeper than cheerleading or a temporary emotional high. When leaders are truly passionate, people feel included in the leader's commitment, part of making important things happen. That's satisfying on a very deep level, and it lasts.

Indeed, creating a lasting impact on those we lead can only stem from passion. The greater the passion, the greater the impact. So, ask yourself this: what fires have you kindled in the hearts of others because of the inferno in yours?

What fires have you kindled in the hearts of others because of the inferno in yours?

WHAT OTHERS HAD TO SAY

"Comic book fans have loved Wolverine, and all the X-Men *characters, for more than the action. I think that's what set it apart from many of the other comic books. In the case of Wolverine, when he appeared, he was a revolution really. He was the first anti-hero."*

–HUGH JACKMAN, ACTOR

"It's the one thing I'm most known for when I go around the world. Most people in the street go, 'Wolverine!' They know I'm Wolverine more than they know Hugh Jackman."

–HUGH JACKMAN, ACTOR

"The way I always describe Wolverine is, if you walked into Logan's room at the X-Mansion, you'd be immediately struck that the room would be split almost literally in half. One would be a total shithole: clothes on the couch, beer cans wherever. This is a guy who doesn't give a damn about anything; he just tosses it. There's nothing sophisticated, nothing respectful; it's altogether creepy. And then there's the other half of the room, which is pristine, elegant, down to the bare essentials of what, for him, is life: a samurai short sword sitting on a desk, and maybe a few precious other items. You'd look at that side of the room and be instantly struck by the balance, the sensitivity. That's the two sides of Logan."

–CHRIS CLAREMONT, WRITER

"Ultimately, this series allowed viewers to enjoy a guy being put in charge who should never be in charge. So to support that, we gave Wolverine some real struggles with being a leader. I never understood why some people couldn't get behind that."

–GREG JOHNSON, HEAD WRITER OF *WOLVERINE* AND *THE X-MEN* TV SERIES

Wolverine #16 (2011) had a humorous take on the clawed Canuck as one of its pages showed some of the best superheroes of the Marvel Universe give their opinion of him. Their opinions were as varied as they were insightful.

Check it out here: http://www.ufunk.net/en/universgeek/what-super-heroes-think-about-wolverine/

CHAPTER 9
THE ORACLE
THE BEHIND-THE-SCENES
INFORMATION BROKER AND LIAISON

★　　★　　★　　★　　★

"I'm Oracle; I know everybody."

—BARBARA GORDON

CHARACTER BIO

Barbara Gordon began her superhero career as Batgirl. Batgirl first appeared in Detective Comics #359, titled *The Million Dollar Debut of Batgirl!* (1967). She was introduced as the daughter of Gotham City police commissioner James Gordon. Her character is said to have a doctorate in library science, and she is employed as head of Gotham City Public Library. Throughout the course of her history, Oracle's (Barbara Gordon) intelligence has been one of her defining attributes.

A tragic event affected the destiny of Barbara Gordon (Batgirl) in 1988. *The Killing Joke*, by Alan Moore (pencilled by Brian Bolland) is perhaps one of the most influential one-shot superhero comic books ever written. The story is deeply psychological and soul stirring. In it, Barbara Gordon is shot point blank by the Joker. This tragic event changed the character (and comic books) forever. In the wake of her shooting, Barbara Gordon lost the use of her legs.

After being crippled by the Joker, she decided to hang up her cowl and instead became a hacker and information broker, calling herself Oracle. Recognizing she could no longer be the kind of superhero she had been, she instead devoted all her time to developing one of the world's most complex and powerful computer systems and set to work accumulating information. She put together a team of crime fighters called the Birds of Prey, showing that she could still fight crime, even from a wheelchair. And succeed she did, earning herself the reputation of the go-to person for contacts or information in the superhero community.

Author Brian Cronin, in *Was Superman A Spy?: And Other Comic Book Legends Revealed* (2009), notes that following the publication of *The Killing Joke*, Barbara Gordon—in her new persona as Oracle—became "more popular, in fact, than she was when she was Batgirl. She even gained her own title, *Birds of Prey*, about her and a group of superhero operatives she organizes." The character has been the subject of analysis in academia, regarding the portrayal of women, librarians, and those living with disabilities in mainstream media. She became a true sociological case study and an inspiration to many.

According to *BusinessWeek*, she is one of the top ten most intelligent fictional superheroes appearing in American comics and is the only female character to appear on the list. She is described by Gail Simone (writer of *Birds of Prey*) as the most intelligent member of the Batman family and all characters having operated out of Gotham City. Not too shabby, huh?

Unfortunately, DC Comics opted to forgo Oracle by giving Barbara the use of her legs again. Following this "miraculous" recovery, she soon reprised her role as Batgirl. For many, Oracle was a better character than Batgirl, not only for what she espoused and represented as a paraplegic, but also for what she contributed, which was far more than acrobatics and martial arts. Her impact was not only felt in the comic industry, but on a sociological scale as well. She has been missed ever since.

LEADERSHIP STYLE

Someone in a wheelchair can't hide his weaknesses; it is obvious to everyone. That, among other things, keeps Oracle real. She doesn't hide behind a mask. She is as genuine as they come. And, perhaps because of her ordeal, she is also very deep, spiritual even:

> You know, at the end of the day, when you close the door and you're all alone . . . And you strip off your armor and lower your guard and peel away the mask . . . When there's nobody watching and nothing to hide . . . And you no longer need to be strong or clever or pretty or brave . . . There's just you. That's it. That's the soul.

—BARBARA GORDON (ORACLE), *BATGIRL* VOL. 1, #45

Now that's keeping it real—and deep at the same time. And that genuineness is apparent in her relationships. Her sincerity and resilience in the face of adversity has earned her the respect, if not the admiration, of her peers. Oracle's vision as a leader is far-reaching. She set her sight on a goal and attained it. When she founded the Birds of Prey, she got support because others saw the value in her vision. Black Canary and the Huntress, who are strong female leads in their own right, decided to work for her and with her, to follow her lead—even if she was in a wheelchair. That says a lot about Barbara. Leadership is influence, and through her skill as Oracle, she has developed into one of the most influential leaders in the super-hero community. What she does, nobody else can do as well. That's what sets her apart. That's what makes others want to follow her. The loss of her legs forced her to reinvent herself and, as surprising as it is, that's when she really came into her own.

So, what does she do exactly? Well, prior to the character's career as a vigilante, Barbara Gordon developed many technological skills, including vast knowledge of computers and electronics, expert skills as a hacker, and graduate training in library sciences. Babs (as known to her friends) is written as having a genius-level intellect and naturally possessing a photographic memory. She is said to read dozens of the world's top newspapers and magazines daily. She is also constantly gathering information from other, less public sources, such as the CIA mainframe, not to mention the data networks of the FBI, NSA, and Interpol (all without their knowledge or consent). As Oracle, Barbara Gordon places her considerable skills and knowledge at the disposal of many of the DC Universe's heroes. As a highly skilled hacker, she is capable of retrieving and dispersing information from private satellites, military installations, and government files. Batman, himself a genius with a wide knowledge base and access to vast information resources, routinely consults Oracle for assistance. Writer and editor Dennis O'Neil, who first established Oracle as Batman's intellectual equal and source of information, stated that "It was logical for her to be there in Batman's world . . . Batman would need someone like that."

So who are Oracle leaders, outside of comics? They are usually wellsprings of information and intelligence. They are at their best reading, researching, and gathering info behind a computer or, better yet, inside a computer! That's also where they're at their happiest. That said, amazingly, they are also great with people. They are not the proto-typical nerd-type leaders because they are able to combine both skill sets. They network online and in person. They are also very good at using their acquired knowledge to guide their team. They are highly esteemed and looked up to because they care about their team members and know how to add value.

STRENGTHS

Obviously, as far as the character is concerned, rising up to the level she has after being crippled is quite a feat. How Oracle has overcome the limitations of her handicap is something that sets her apart in terms of sheer force of character. In the same way, Oracle leaders are determined. But it's more than that. Oracle leaders are powerful because of their amazing minds and people skills. They are masters at connecting and creating networks of people to work with, and they are also masters at connecting with computer networks as well. Imagine a computer expert . . . with powerful drive, vision, great emotional insight, and insane people skills to boot! Hard to conceive, isn't it? Well, that's an Oracle leader in a nutshell. Whether they be male or female, they marry both great technical knowledge with leadership ability—a rare and coveted skill set indeed!

WEAKNESSES

Being the smartest person in the class has great advantages, but it also has its down side. Genius-level intellects the likes of Oracle leaders can often find themselves alienated and lonely. This may or may not be why they like spending so much time with tech. So, is it the chicken or the egg? Do they like spending time on intellectual pursuits because they feel alienated, or do they feel alienated because they are invested in intellectual pursuits? Your guess is as good as mine.

EFFICIENCY RATING

In today's high tech world where leadership is more and more people oriented and less and less task oriented, the skill set of Oracle leaders is hard to beat. A twenty-year study of leadership effectiveness conducted by Stanford University's School of Business concluded that about 15 percent of one's success in leading organizations comes from technical skills and knowledge, while 85 percent comes from the ability to connect with people and engender trust and mutual understanding. Oracle leaders cover the whole spectrum. They are tech-smart, intuitive-type leaders who are perfectly equipped to deal with the demands of today's corporate world and complex human relations. You need to update your website? They can do it. You need to bring your team together? Consider it done. You need to resolve workplace conflict? They can handle that too. They can even hack into a rival company's computer and engage in corporate spying—not that they would ever resort to it, but they could if they wanted.

PEOPLE SKILLS: 10

SMARTS: 10

VISION: 8

CHARACTER: 9

ADAPTABILITY: 10

FOCUS: 9

"IT" FACTOR: 9

OVERALL: 9

CALL TO ACTION: BE GRITTY AND TECH-SAVVY

*"A little over a year has passed since my old life ended, since I died
and was reborn. The shadows remain, but only to give contrast to the light. I
am no longer a distaff impersonation of someone else. I am me—
more me than I have ever been. My life is my own. I embrace it,
and the light, with a deep, continuing joy."*

—BARBARA GORDON, *ORACLE YEAR ONE: BORN OF HOPE*

Everybody suffers setbacks and trials in life. Our attitude towards
them is what will either make us or break us. In fact, the greatest
leaders around us are those who have developed a knack for overcoming obstacles. They are determined and gritty. Those who have
fallen down and gotten back up, who have failed and yet kept trying,
they are the ones we look up to the most. After all, when you lead,
you have to be able to get your team through the tough patches,
right? Some of us, like Oracle, look at a trial and say, "How can I get
through this? What can I do to make the most of this situation? I
will not let this cripple me (literally)!"

Initially, Barbara was determined to prove to Batman, and the world, that there should be a Batgirl. He didn't make it easy on her, yet she proved him wrong. This alone was no small feat. How often do we get discouraged when our friends and families discourage us from pursuing our goals and dreams? Pursuing our dreams gets tougher when discouragement comes from someone we admire— as was the case for her.

As Oracle, she proved to the world that superheroes don't need to wear capes . . . or to even walk! Her determination didn't stop at accepting her new reality; it went as far as forging a new one. She didn't just overcome an obstacle, she took that obstacle and made it into a stepping stone towards a greater ideal. Talk about making lemons into lemonade!

"The measure of our leadership is greatly determined by what measures we take in confronting our difficult circumstances."

We all have our own challenges and obstacles. How we deal with them is the measure of what we are made of. Whether in life or at work, just like Oracle, the measure of our leadership is greatly determined by what measures we take in confronting our difficult circumstances. Are you facing a challenge or difficulty? Are you overcoming your trials, or are you crippled by them? Keep in mind that trials are hurdles which stand between how you are and how great you can be. Our ability as human beings to overcome trials is greatly formative. Some ordeals can be extremely daunting. They can scar our body, soul, and psyche. But remember this: your scars are an indication that you overcame whatever tried to harm you. Like Oracle, you can and should harness your greatness from your setbacks. Unlike Oracle, most of us are lucky enough to be able to walk after our battles.

Another thing that we can learn from Oracle is keeping up to date with tech. Are your computer skills lacking? We live in a tech-savvy world where it is becoming increasingly important to master technology. Whether it be purchasing the latest iPhone app or applying all your knowledge in such a way that tech will work with you and for you, owning your skills with the latest tech is not just required, but a must in order to be relevant as a leader in today's modern world. You don't have to become a computer know-it-all, but you should keep up with it at the very least.

> "Owning your skills with the latest tech is not just required, but a must in order to be relevant as a leader in today's modern world."

Keeping pace with tech is vital in today's economy. A case in point and cautionary tale is the demise of photography giant Kodak. They procrastinated to get on the digital camera bandwagon, and they lost everything. Although they actually invented digital cameras (Kodak engineer Steve Sasson invented the first digital camera in 1975), their procrastination in making this technology a priority ahead of traditional photography while the iron was hot (early 2000s) brought massive failure. They did eventually go fully digital, but it was too little too late, and in 2012 an American giant fell as a result. It was a Kodak moment not soon to be forgotten. Thus we can learn from this and be more like Oracle, making tech an integral part of our leadership and making it our ally in order to remain relevant.

WHAT OTHERS HAD TO SAY

"Some yes, some no. But many of the great stories remain. For example—Batgirl. The Killing Joke still happened and she was Oracle. Now she will go through physical rehabilitation and become a more seasoned and nuanced character because she had these incredible and diverse experiences."

—DC COMICS' "THE NEW 52 AND YOU" EMAIL SENT TO RETAILERS

"We had hordes of people in spandex beating up criminals . . . We didn't have anybody like Oracle, who overcame a disability."

—DENNIS O'NEIL, WRITER

"She's fantastic because even just sitting in a chair in a dark room by herself, she's tremendously compelling. The DCU without her would be a much less interesting place."

—GAIL SIMONE, WRITER

"Over the last decade, Oracle has shown the power of a strong network of contacts, and in doing so she shows Business Superheroes the importance of cultivating contacts and developing assets that can further their collective goals."

—SEAN WISE, AUTHOR OF *HOW TO BE A BUSINESS SUPERHERO*

CHAPTER 10
THE NICK FURY
THE STRONG AND DEDICATED
POSITIONAL LEADER

"I recognize the council has made a decision, but given that it's a stupid-a** decision, I've elected to ignore it."

—NICK FURY

CHARACTER BIO

Colonel Nicholas Joseph "Nick" Fury was created by the iconic duo of artist Jack Kirby and writer Stan Lee. Fury first appeared in *Sgt. Fury and His Howling Commandos* #1 (May 1963), a World War II combat series that portrayed the cigar-smoking Fury as leader of an elite US Army unit. Fury, in the comics and movies, is portrayed as one of the greatest strategic minds in the world, a gifted leader and a master of espionage.

The Nick Fury most of us are familiar with, however, is the one portrayed by Samuel L. Jackson in the Marvel movies on the big screen. This modern rendition, portrayed as an African American (he was originally Caucasian), came to be in the Ultimate Marvel Continuity. Because the character portrayed by Jackson in the films was so recognizable, Marvel almost retired the original character, replacing him with his African American son, Nick Fury Jr., who, like the Ultimate Marvel version, is patterned on Jackson.

He is the appointed Director of S.H.I.E.L.D. (Strategic Homeland Intervention, Enforcement, and Logistics Division). The acronym previously stood for Strategic Hazard Intervention Espionage Logistics Directorate and, originally, Supreme Headquarters, International Espionage, Law-Enforcement Division. In any case, it's a mouthful and thank goodness for acronyms. It's basically the Marvel rendition of the ultimate super-secret government agency. I could tell you more about it, but then I'd have to kill you.

LEADERSHIP STYLE

"His name is Fury. Nick Fury. He has been many things in this life. Currently, he is commander-in-chief of S.H.I.E.L.D., making sure when we go to sleep at night . . . we wake up in the land of the free."

—AVENGERS VOL. 2, #3

That's Nick Fury in a nutshell. If following orders of his superiors will contribute to us waking up in a relatively safe world everyday, he will gladly do what he's told. If it goes against it, however, he just will not comply.

In his position as director of S.H.I.E.L.D., Nick Fury is one of the most powerful men in the world. This is largely because of what he knows, what he has access to, and who he has access to. In spite of his massive influence, he models remarkable trustworthiness and integrity in his functions. We've all heard power corrupts and absolute power corrupts absolutely. Well, although Fury is no angel, he didn't become corrupt as a result of his ranking. That, by the way, is one of the biggest challenges for positional leaders (i.e., leaders who have authority through an assigned position). Since they are given the position and influence of a leader, they didn't necessarily have to earn it by gaining a following. That, in itself, has made many crappy leaders, indeed. Simon Sinek, author of *Why Leaders Eat Last*, had this to say on the matter: "Leadership is neither a rank, nor a title. It is a choice. The choice to provide care and protection for those for whom we are responsible."

And Nick Fury does this very well. Although he leads super-powered beings, who, for the most part, don't need his protection, he exemplifies that very attitude for the sake of his team members. Not becoming complacent and corrupt as a result of his title is Fury's biggest accomplishment.

Fury is not perfect; he has lied to his team members on occasion. This was either because he wasn't in the know—the council (his superiors) had lied to him—or because he felt he needed to lie in order to protect his team. Nevertheless, it is not something he resorts to lightly.

What makes him stand out as a leader is also how he can masterfully put together a team like The Avengers and then get out of their way to let them work. Leading a group of super-gifted individuals like The Avengers is a tough job, and Fury pulls it off by giving them enough leeway to perform at their peak. He knows what needs to be done; he tells them, but then he lets his team figure out how they're going to do it. He has fully understood that great leaders do not know everything and that they do not need to know everything. In fact, he has understood you need to rely on those under you, your field agents, those who are in the grind, in the trenches, to fill you in. They provide valuable knowledge and info the leader needs, and he uses that to his advantage. This is a valuable and rare trait among positional leaders. Fury-type leaders know the "why" better than anyone else. Ralph Waldo Emerson put it this way: "The man who knows how will always have a job. The man who knows why will always be his boss."

And that's why Fury is in charge: he knows why. He even tells Captain America what to do! Ultimately, his "why" is pretty big: preserving the security of America and the world. He's got broad shoulders to carry this load, but he knows better than anyone how to surround himself with the right people to help him with that.

We need more Nick Fury leaders out there. These guys find a way to shine in a positional role or title, which is no small feat. Give them a team, and they will lead them exceptionally well. Give them superiors, and they will follow their instructions with care, promptness, and effectiveness. Give them underhanded projects to accomplish . . . and believe it, they will give you hell.

> *"There was an idea called The Avengers Initiative. The idea was to bring together a group of remarkable people so they could become something more. See if they could work together when we needed them to fight the battles we never could."*
>
> **—NICK FURY**

Well done, Mr. Fury. Well done.

STRENGTHS

Nick Fury-type leaders have many strengths in their leadership arsenal. They have knowledge, connections, vast experience, and are great managers. They are great at organizing their teams and delegating. Their strongest asset, though, as a positional leader, is how they masterfully bridge the gap between their superiors and those under them. Not only do they relay the information that is needed for the team to be efficient, but they also never compromise the project itself by giving away too much information—to the great pleasure of their superiors. They appeal to both sides, most of the time. But what makes the Fury leaders even more commendable is how, if needed, they will dare to confront those above them in order to protect those under them. How they inspire trust, confidence, and safety for their team members is what sets them apart.

WEAKNESSES

The main chink in the armor of Fury-type leaders is the fact that they have a title, a position. This requires them to operate within the confines of set regulations that might not always be in the best interest of the people they serve. Positional leaders have limitations that are intrinsically linked to their title. The organization or company they work for set down the rules they must abide by. Sometimes, this corporate philosophy is good. Most of the time, however, it is interest driven and not people driven. This puts these types of leaders in awkward positions, no matter how well intentioned they are.

EFFICIENCY RATING

> *"It's not the position that makes the leader, but the leader that makes the position."*

—STANLEY HUFFTY

I have worked for positional leaders most of my life; some were good, most were not. It is sad to say, but positional leaders are destined to disappoint. In all fairness, though, those who lacked mostly did so because of their failure to dance between the two extremes of obeying their superiors and leading their team in a way that inspired trust. That is what positional leadership requires, and that is what makes it such a challenge. It is also the most common type of corporate leadership, and the one most of us have come to know, whether by wearing the mantle or following someone who did. These are the guys (and gals) most of us refer to as "boss." We could say that Nick Fury-type leaders have made an art of positional leadership. They have mastered it in all that it has to offer and made the most of all of its inherent shortcomings.

PEOPLE SKILLS: 8

SMARTS: 9

VISION: 9

CHARACTER: 9

ADAPTABILITY: 6

FOCUS: 10

"IT" FACTOR: 9

OVERALL: 8

CALL TO ACTION: STAND STRONG

Integrity is achievable through conviction. Compromising between your superiors and your team members doesn't mean compromising with your values or not standing up for your beliefs. You can be a great supervisor, boss, or manager, in spite of the challenges your title brings, by modelling fairness, integrity, and decisiveness.

This call to action is mainly for positional leaders. I had the opportunity to ask one experienced supervisor I worked with about the biggest challenges for a positional leader. He was gracious enough to give me some feedback and confirmed exactly what I wrote in this chapter (i.e., having to operate within the confines of set regulations that might not always be in the best interest of the people they serve is the biggest downside). If the company's philosophy sucks, their leadership usually sucks. When I asked him about the upside of positional leadership, he had to ponder for a moment (understandably). And then he surprised me by saying this: "Your role is more defined. That way you know exactly what is expected of you on a day-to-day basis—that is, if you are on the lower leadership rung of the ladder. If you go higher up in your position, your goals are set week to week or month to month. The higher you go, the longer term the objectives."

The liabilities of being a positional leader are, as follows:

★ They operate within the confines of their position and do not usually look to make an impact outside of it.

★ They are usually not visionary, and not required to be. Rather, they carry out someone else's vision.

★ They are not usually employee or people oriented. Rather, they are required to be task oriented.

★ Usually, positional leaders will influence employees through their position, rather than their influence.

★ Communication with their staff is on a need-to-know basis, rather than intentional and relationship oriented.

Whichever rung you find yourself at, if this is your job, let me ask you a question: Do you make it your business to become the best positional leader around? Do you strive to be a great representative for the organization you work for, or do you just take your position for granted? The positional leader has the dual responsibility of being a follower and a leader at the same time. He acts as a bridge between the employees and upper management. As a bridge, how solid are you? What are the values that constitute your philosophy? Are you tossed to and fro, between the whims of upper management and the complaints of employees, or are you firm, rock solid, yet fair in your decisiveness? What are the values that constitute your philosophy? Your philosophy and values are going to determine how strong you stand. As the saying goes, if you don't stand for something, you will fall for anything. The greatest challenge of positional leadership is proving that you deserve your position by exemplifying genuine leadership. And that requires intentionality.

> "Your philosophy and values are going to determine
> ,how strong you stand. As the saying goes, if you don't stand
> for something, you will fall for anything."

What if, in your capacity as a leader, you intentionally became the best "boss" possible—someone others trust and appreciate, someone they know they can talk to about any problem? Are you someone who makes them feel safe? The good positional leader should concentrate on one main thing: set the objective and then step back and watch it happen. Ask yourself this: would they follow me if I didn't have this position? If the answer is yes, good. Keep improving and don't let up. If the answer is no, however, you really need to look at yourself in the mirror. It could be you need to work on improving your leadership skills. Standing strong like Nick Fury is not for the faint of heart.

WHAT OTHERS HAD TO SAY

"They are working on The Fantastic Four, The Silver Surfer, Iron Man, Dr. Strange, The Hulk—they're doing a sequel to Spider-Man, a sequel to X-Men, and probably a third sequel to Blade. They still haven't gotten around to Nick Fury, Agent of S.H.I.E.L.D. . . . "

—STAN LEE, *DAREDEVIL* MOVIE PREMIERE, 2003

"I just happened to be in a comic store, and I picked up the comic because I saw my face. And I was like, 'Wait a minute, I'm not sure I remember giving somebody permission to use my image."

—SAMUEL L. JACKSON, ACTOR, ON THE DEPICTION OF NICK FURY IN 2002'S *THE ULTIMATES* #1

"The first thing I said was I hope you don't mind me completely exploiting your appearance in my book thirteen years back, and he said, "F**k, no, man. Thanks for the 9 picture deal."

—MARK MILLAR, WRITER, WHEN HE MET SAMUEL L. JACKSON

"When he talks to Cap, he can talk to Cap in several different ways. He can talk to him as an equal, in terms of they were both soldiers from a specific era, and you understand his kind of morality. He can also talk to him as a guy who's part of a world he doesn't know anything about, and he's a mentor now to help him do something. And then I speak to him sometimes as a boss."

—SAMUEL L. JACKSON, ACTOR

CHAPTER 11

THE PROFESSOR X
THE RECRUITING, TEACHING, AND MENTORING LEADER

"Just because someone stumbles and loses their path,
doesn't mean they're lost forever."

—CHARLES XAVIER

CHARACTER BIO

Professor Charles Francis Xavier (aka Professor X) is the founder and leader of the X-Men in Marvel Comics. He was created by none other than writer Stan Lee and artist Jack Kirby. He first appeared in *The X-Men* #1 (September 1963). An interesting and little known fact is that Stan Lee once stated that the physical inspiration of Professor Xavier was from Academy Award–winning actor Yul Brynner. Professor Xavier's character development has also been inspired by Martin Luther King Jr. Later, in 1996, writer Scott Lobdell established Xavier's middle name to be Francis in *Uncanny X-Men* #328. For most of us, though, Charles Xavier was immortalized on the big screen through his incarnation by Patrick Stewart. When Stewart auditioned to play the part, they showed him a comic book with Professor X on the cover, and he said, "What am I doing on the front of a comic book?"

Professor X's origin story is quite detailed and intricate. Charles Francis Xavier was born in New York City to the wealthy Brian Xavier, a well-respected nuclear scientist, and Sharon Xavier. After his father died in an accident, everything fell apart for young Charles. Nevertheless, in spite of a troubled childhood in a blended family, Xavier managed to get a top-grade education under his belt. Of course, his vast intellect and telepathic powers helped just a wee bit. In the end, he graduated with honors at the age of sixteen from Harvard University. He also attended other schools where he received PhDs in genetics, biophysics, psychology, and anthropology, with a two-year residence at Pembroke College, Oxford University. He also received an MD in psychiatry while spending some years in London. I'm guessing his doctorate thesis must have been on the psychology of overachievers—just saying.

In the comics, he lost the use of his legs because an alien villain named Lucifer (no apparent relation to his biblical counterpart) dropped a huge rock on him. In spite of his handicap, Xavier remains one of the most powerful mutants on earth. His mutant abilities were made manifest to him while living with his mother, stepfather, and stepbrother. His stepbrother Marko used to beat him up. In retribution, his father secretly beat him—and young Charles felt his half-sibling's pain firsthand, thanks to the emergence of his mutant telepathic powers.

Xavier's powers go as follows: He is able to perceive the thoughts of others or project his own thoughts within a radius of approximately four hundred kilometers, or more if he wishes. He can learn foreign languages by reading the language centers of the brain of someone adept and alternately can "teach" languages to others in the same manner. His vast psionic powers also enable him to manipulate the mind of others in various ways. He can warp perceptions to make himself seem invisible, project mental illusions, cause loss of particular memories or total amnesia, inflict pain, and induce temporary mental and/or physical paralysis in others.

When Xavier witnessed the gradual emergence of many more mutants (super-powered humans) like him, he became convinced they should not only learn to control their powers, but also use them for the good of humanity. This is why, out of sheer altruism, he founded Xavier's School for Gifted Youngsters (later named the Xavier Institute) to teach mutants to explore and control their powers. Even though the general public and the government have shown much hostility towards mutants in the Marvel continuity, Xavier still holds to his ideal that mutants and ordinary humans can peacefully co-exist. Making this dream come true is his life's work and his purpose. Just like Martin Luther King Jr., after whom he was modelled, he has a dream!

LEADERSHIP STYLE

Charles Xavier is the kind of leader who is fully invested in recruiting, teaching, and molding the next generation of leaders. That's his passion. He has a knack for finding (through Cerebro, a technology which enhances his telepathic powers) those who need his one-of-a-kind education, services, and training. But he is also smart in going about it. You see, he doesn't just seek out birds with a broken wing in order to help them heal. He makes sure that they can also, in turn, become key people who will aid in his mission. What he really wants is a win-win for both his recruits and his mission. He loves to invest time and energy into new prospects who show promise. He loves to teach and is passionate about seeing others come into their own. He loves reaching out to the next generation of mutants. His great mind-reading ability also enables him to know which recruits will pan out. His gift has allowed him to recruit, train, and prepare many good leaders, including Cyclops, Storm, Jean Grey, Nightcrawler, Beast, and Wolverine, to name a few.

Although their passion is forming new leaders, Professor X leaders go about it with great care and insight. They don't just take anybody under their wing. They are welcoming and non-judgmental, but they are choosy. It was Jim Rohn who said, "Talk about things that matter to people who care."

Professor X leaders know to do just that. They are masters at targeting the right individuals to recruit. They have a knack for knowing when to push, when to pull back, and when to let go. It is an art that comes through great EQ and intuition. In that respect, they do seem to have some sort of telepathic powers. Good leadership and mentoring involves knowing the boundaries that exist when teaching and training. They are very wise teachers and very patient. If they believe in you, they can put up with many of your failures and won't give up easily on you. They get a kick out of seeing you figure things out on your own. They are very altruistic and thrive on seeing others succeed. This trait alone proves how confident they are in their own abilities. They don't feel threatened by others' successes.

Recruiters, headhunters, teachers, coaches, placement agents, and trainers—those are the positions Professor X leaders flock to and thrive in. Any job where they can recruit, connect at a deeper level, and teach others is a good fit for them. They love people more than projects. For the Professor X leader, the workers are the work; people are their projects. They understand the value of human resources and act accordingly. When a Professor X leader is the head of an organization, he always makes sure the company's philosophy is built around making its workers happy. His personal philosophy is built with and around people—a rare and valued thing indeed in the corporate world.

STRENGTHS

Professor X made the list of *BusinessWeek's* May 2006 top ten smartest comic book characters (at number nine). Yes, he has genius-level intellect. In the same manner, Professor X leaders in our communities and workplaces are very smart men and women. They have to be. You cannot train, teach, coach, and mentor if you don't have the knowledge to back it up. They are passionate about what they do and excel at it too. Their love of people and seeing others grow and come into their own sets them apart. They are experienced, kind, and, despite not having telepathic powers, extremely intuitive, intelligent, and empathetic. They espouse the Law of Empowerment, which states that "only secure leaders give power to others." Comic book writer Joss Whedon observed, "Recognizing power in another does not diminish your own." In fact, it makes you a better person and empowers you in the process. Professor X leaders understand and apply this principle superbly!

WEAKNESSES

In the same way that Xavier can feel the pain of other people, Professor X leaders are vulnerable to the pains that come through deep human connections. The ties they build with others make them more emotionally vulnerable than most of the other leaders described in this book. The role of recruiter, coach, and mentor brings investment in others that goes deeper than simple training. They actually care for their protégés and, in doing so, make themselves more emotionally vulnerable. In the event of strife, rejection, or downright betrayal, the cut goes deeper. When you care for people, you make yourself vulnerable to them.

EFFICIENCY RATING

Professor X leaders are great across the board. They are connected emotionally, and their EQs are very high. Their intuitive people skills and patience make them highly respected leaders. The greatest leaders are those who are able to empower others and make them into leaders. This is the quality that makes Professor X leaders so valuable.

PEOPLE SKILLS: 10

SMARTS: 10

VISION: 10

CHARACTER: 9

ADAPTABILITY: 8

FOCUS: 10

"IT" FACTOR: 9

OVERALL: 9

CALL TO ACTION: ADD VALUE TO PEOPLE BY VALUING THEM

"If your vision is for a year, plant wheat. If your vision is for ten years, plant trees. If your vision is for a lifetime, plant people."

—CHINESE PROVERB

As leaders, our lives and purposes are constantly about engaging people. And the best way to engage people is to show them you care, to add value to them. Investing time, money, and resources in employees and staff is the best investment any leader can make. As we all know, the days when someone spends his whole life with one company are pretty much over. But if those who come through your organization come out better when they leave, it means you have added to their measure. Not only have you invested in their future, but in the foundation of your company as well. Also, chances are, if they feel valued, they will not want to leave. When an organization implements a healthy philosophy of growth and learning, it secures its future success. The customer is important, but many companies neglect the workers in the process of pleasing their customers. That's just plain wrong.

In the first *X-Men* movie by Brian Singer, Wolverine was brought to Xavier's school after he had sustained injuries in a violent encounter. The example, patience, care, and teaching given by Professor X (and the lovely Jean Grey) to the feral mutant made him forego his lone wolf stance and join the X-Men to aid their cause. He later even convinced Rogue, who ran away from the mansion, to go back and stick it out.

Professor X leader types make others feel valued and cared for, no matter how different they are. They always see the potential in people, not their differences or faults. This is extremely attractive to people. Who wouldn't want to be around someone who makes them feel good about themselves and empowers them? As Dale Carnegie says in *How to Win Friends and Influence People*, "You can make more friends in two months by becoming interested in other people than you can in two years by trying to get other people interested in you."

Professor X leaders aim to build up people through their teaching and coaching process. A wise and experienced leader will aim to reproduce himself, to make others into leaders as well. When you add value to people, you empower them to come into their own. If you tell a man he is strong, you help him become so. All the great leaders of history had someone who helped and inspired them. Johann Wolfgang von Goethe summed it up nicely with these wise words: "When we treat man as he is, we make him worse than he is. When we treat him as if he already was what he potentially could be, we make him what he should be."

"When you add value to people, you empower them to come into their own. If you tell a man he is strong, you help him become so."

Leadership is influence. Do you make a habit of being a positive influence on others? Do you aim to add value to them by encouraging, inspiring, teaching, and coaching them? The best possible way to build up your own success as a leader is through building up others.

WHAT OTHERS HAD TO SAY

*"I was your most helpless student, and you unlocked my mind.
You showed me what I was, you showed me who I could be."*

—WOLVERINE, TO CHARLES XAVIER

*"Playing Professor Xavier was restricting. In fact, for a couple of days
Brian [Singer] had been saying to me 'Less, less. Do less. You're loud.
You're speaking too loudly. Quieter, quieter.'"*

—PATRICK STEWART, ACTOR

*"Professor Xavier always talks about engaging, always talks about going to
the community, and a lot of people really need to pay attention to these comic
books, because I think we can learn a lot from them."*

—OMEKONGO DIBINGA, MOTIVATIONAL SPEAKER

*"That's really the key to him in this one, that his power, which has always
been seen as his psychic ability or great intelligence or whatever, really what I
think it is [is] empathy. That's his greatest power."*

—JAMES MCAVOY, ACTOR

CHAPTER 12

THE AQUAMAN
THE COMMITTED INHERITOR OF HIGH-STAKES LEADERSHIP

"I've worked hard to earn the respect and trust of every living creature beneath the waves—and I take my job very seriously . . . I'm Aquaman, King of the Seven Seas . . . and I'm the best!"

—AQUAMAN

CHARACTER BIO

Aquaman, the King of the Seven Seas, King of Atlantis! A highly underrated superhero if ever there were one, he was created by Paul Norris and Mort Weisinger and debuted in *More Fun Comics* #73 (November 1941).

Aquaman's origin story has been retold, revamped, and tweaked a few times since his creation. But here are the main lines that define the character for posterity. First off, he is a hero caught between two kingdoms, two worlds. He is half-human and half-Atlantean hybrid. And don't kid yourself; he is a lot more than just a guy who "talks to fish."

Aquaman (aka Arthur Curry) was the son of Atlanna, an Atlantean princess banished from Atlantis due to her interest in and frequent visits to the surface world (think the Little Mermaid), and Tom Curry, a surface man and lighthouse keeper. One night, during a very bad storm, Tom Curry found Atlanna washed up on the shore by storm-tossed waves. He rescued her from harm. Shortly thereafter, Curry and Atlanna made the lighthouse their home. They developed a strong bond that eventually led to a romantic relationship. It is from this unorthodox union that Arthur Curry was born.

In the DC animated movie *Aquaman: Throne of Atlantis,* which is basically a telling of his origins and royal calling, we see him, as an adult, find out about his phenomenal powers. These powers include swimming at one hundred miles per hour, communicating telepathically with all manners of sea life, and phenomenal strength and resistance. Unbeknownst to most is that he can lift in excess of sixty tons and has near invulnerability! But what is more is the royal blood that courses through his veins. He later heeds the call to claim the throne of Atlantis as its rightful ruler.

Sadly, for many years, Aquaman was subject to ridicule from comic book fans. He was said to be a lame character and has taken a lot of heat. This is why he was picked as the hero to represent the "responsible inheritor of leadership." Nevertheless, with all of the revamping and changes he has undergone in recent times—thanks in great part to the dedicated writing of Geoff Johns—I believe these underdog years are behind him. That's my opinion anyway. I think he is now a riveting and fascinating character who has been through many, many trials. He lost a son, a wife, and a hand, among other things. And every time he was in over his head, he managed to keep his head above water through sheer determination and perseverance. Yeah, being a great swimmer surely helped with that.

LEADERSHIP STYLE

My wife asked me, "You're talking about inheritors of leadership, so why pick Aquaman over Thor? Didn't Thor inherit leadership? Isn't he a more popular character?" You have to understand; Liz is not that much into superheroes, but she knows movies and recognizes popularity when she sees it. Most everybody knows the Asgardian god has more pull and popularity than the King of the Seven Seas. Thor has had many movies in which he was featured in recent years, but not Aquaman. So why pick Aquaman? Well, there are four reasons:

1. I didn't think my readers could relate that much with a god, and neither could I.

2. I happen to prefer Aquaman.

3. I've always had a soft spot for underdogs.

4. Like Wolverine, I'm not a great swimmer and admire those who are.

That being said, there is just something about blue blood, isn't there? Royalty just does something to a person. It's inherent to the position. Well, think about it. If you were told you descended from a royal bloodline and the kingdom wants you back on the throne, wouldn't it alter the way you carry and perceive yourself? I sure would act differently. I'd be more confident and probably would walk with my head held up higher. The least we can say is that Aquaman really does carry himself like a monarch. He doesn't second-guess himself, and he is very confident—no matter what people say about him. He says what he means, and he means what he says.

In the revamping of the Justice League in *The New 52*, we see a leader who believes he should lead—even on land and even the Justice League! When he first meets the other members of the league, the first thing he asks them is, "So, who's in charge here? I vote me." And later he adds, "You've obviously gathered here to fight them (Darkseid's Parademons). But I don't see a leader . . . I've got some experience with leadership. I'm the rightful heir to the throne of Atlantis. I'm their king."

Some would argue he was being cocky. Perhaps. What I saw was someone who knew how dire and urgent the situation was and offered to guide the team through it. He is direct, but well meaning. As a king, he knows why, and he knows how to address a matter. But more than that, he is used to having others do as he says just because he is the king. That attitude is apparent in his dealings with others. He is decisive and authoritative, and that can sometimes rub people the wrong way. Truthfully, it's their loss. Because when all is said and done, he is a good man, a good leader, and he cares about sea life and earth life very deeply, belonging to both. He takes his kingship and responsibility very seriously, and he wants to make sure he honors that position and everything it entails. He really does carry himself like a king.

The Aquaman leaders out there are those who inherited businesses or organizations. They didn't build them. They didn't start from scratch. They didn't necessarily "climb up the corporate ladder." They were given the reins because either they were born and groomed for it at the onset, because the company belonged to their family, or they came from the outside with the right qualifications and were hired for the top position from the get go.

There is a paradox here. This is great for them, and not so great at the same time. It's a bit like the positional leaders' struggle: once they are given the position, they have to prove they deserve it. It's great in the sense that it secures their future—for it is likely the top-dog position. On the other hand, they can end up with a target on their back because petty people in their organization may see them as "daddy's boy" or "mommy's girl" or whatever else the case may be. This means they have to work, often twice as hard, to earn the respect they deserve. It does test their mettle. This is very much like Aquaman. He inherited the throne of Atlantis after having never lived there. Being made monarch made him a lot of enemies from within the realm. It forces him to prove every day that he deserves to be in charge; he must live up to the position. But Aquaman also has to prove his worth in comicdom, where he has been maligned and mocked as the guy who talks to fish, when, in fact, he is a lot more than that.

We saw what affected the positional leader in an earlier chapter. Although in a similar predicament, the Aquaman leaders of our organizations differ because they are often the sons and daughters and family members of the founders, presidents, and CEOs, and also because they can be outsiders who beat everybody who vied to get the top position. Some of them do the position great honor by establishing themselves as good and strong leaders (like Aquaman), while others might just enjoy a free ride up the corporate ladder because of mommy or daddy or because of a big degree from a fancy university. Unfortunately, we have seen some of these folks make the headlines for all the wrong reasons one too many times. Nuff said.

STRENGTHS

Strong, confident, authoritative, decisive, knowledgeable, and experienced, the Aquaman leaders of this world are, for the most part, very good leaders. They have great knowledge of the inner workings of their organizations and its people because either they grew up in it or have an incredible resume. They are perfect for the position in most cases. They are practical and quick at making decisions. They are able to make those tough decisions and see the big picture. If the family members before them were good leaders, more often than not, they will emulate them.

WEAKNESSES

Sometimes, the sins of the father precede them. These leaders might not have been prepared adequately for this responsibility, or they may inherit a company with big problems. This can be hard to overcome. Other times, since they didn't build or found the company, they can take it for granted and act irresponsibly. There's something about sweating and bleeding for something you're building that will make you respect, honor, and maintain it better. Last but not least, they often have to work very hard before they earn the trust of the people in their organization and are seen as worthy of the mantle.

EFFICIENCY RATING

Aquaman leaders are just like their comic book counterpart: underrated. They can swim with the big boys just as well as most corporate leaders out there. In fact, since most of them bathed in the organization's philosophy and workings from their youth, they tend to know better than most how to work the helm, steer the ship, and chart the course. If they get a lot of bad press, it's mostly because of a few rotten apples. Most of them deserve more credit.

In *The New 52* Justice League, when Aquaman boldly comes on the scene to join the battling heroes, Green Lantern, not liking his bravado, turns to him and tauntingly snaps, "Superman might not say a lot, but he can fly and juggle trucks. The Flash is the fastest man alive. Wonder Woman can slice through an army. And me? I can do anything with this ring. So, really, what can you do that we can't?"

And just as parademons were flying over the water in their direction, Aquaman turned towards the harbour and focused his psychic energy. Immediately, dozens of giant great white sharks jumped out of the water, clamping parademons in their powerful jaws, and crushing them. One of them evaded the shark attack and was still headed for the heroes. Aquaman grabbed his trident and, with a quick upward motion, planted it in the creature's head from the neck up, killing it instantly. A truly impressive and grandiose feat. As the creature fell on the dock, Green Lantern, almost speechless, said, "Never mind." Yes, good Aquaman leaders let their actions speak louder than their words. That's how they silence their detractors.

PEOPLE SKILLS: 7

SMARTS: 8

VISION: 9

CHARACTER: 9

ADAPTABILITY: 9

FOCUS: 9

"IT" FACTOR: 7

OVERALL: 8

CALL TO ACTION: BE COMMITTED AND RESPONSIBLE

In most instances, these leaders have big shoes to fill, and their every move is scrutinized. Those who inherit the mantle of leadership as top dog of an organization, like Aquaman did when he inherited the Throne of Atlantis, have huge responsibilities. In the face of such demands, there are those who step up, and those who, well, don't. The character and attitude of Aquaman leaders determine how they fare after the torch has been passed to them. In the comics, Aquaman rises to the challenge and honors the title of king bestowed upon him. He sees its importance and the honor associated with it and is determined to lead Atlantis in such a way that the kingdom will thrive.

Merriam-Webster defines *responsibility* as "a duty or task that you are required or expected to do; something that you should do because it is morally right, legally required, etc." And commitment: "the state or quality of being dedicated to a cause, activity, etc."

Commitment and responsibility are key elements of leadership. They are intrinsically part of it. Anybody who wants to lead is, in fact, saying, "I want to take on more responsibility." Simon Sinek said, "Leadership is not a license to do less; it is a responsibility to do more."

"Commitment and responsibility are key elements of leadership. They are intrinsically part of it. Anybody who wants to lead is, in fact, saying, "I want to take on more responsibility."

The heavy load thrust upon Aquaman leaders' shoulders are what makes them or breaks them. Their character and willingness to grab hold of responsibility will determine if their team will embrace them or reject them. They are expected to justify their position more so than ordinary positional leaders because they inherit a bigger role and they are seen as being even more undeserving than those who go through the normal hiring process or rung climbing. This fact is observable especially for those who were handed the position because of their birthright and not necessarily because of any past accomplishments. Understandably, this makes their ascent to respectability more arduous, scrutinized, and criticized.

In the event that they do have past accomplishments under their belt, it makes for a much smoother transition. The player who has already scored a few touchdowns for the team is much more welcome than the one who signed a multi-million-dollar deal before he even ran one lap with them. In that respect, the family member who signs the company away to them has a big hand in whether or not the Aquaman leader succeeds or not. It is always better if he made the candidate go through a natural learning process in the trenches than if he appoints them the title of President or CEO without the candidate having served there.

So, are you an Aquaman leader? Were you given a great title or position out of the blue? Did you inherit a family business? If yes, now what? What will you do with the immense privilege and responsibility you were given? Will you be caring, teachable, and dutiful? Or will you be complacent, careless, and arrogant? Will you honor or dishonor your title? There are a few things you can do to treat your inheritance in a responsible way and with the respect it deserves:

1. Be your own (Aqua) man: Become an entrepreneur in your own right by seeking training, earning credentials, and gathering experience by doing the business, not just being the business. Prove you can swim with the big boys by seeking to improve.

2. What's in a name? Don't rely on your name to get by. You can use the name, but thrive on reinforcing it, on improving it by your sound decisions and actions. Make that name reputable for another generation of peers, clients, and employees.

3. Don't use the business's resources as your own. Sure, you were given access to family riches, but treat it as you would any other business. Treat it as if you built it through blood and tears. Get it to grow and expand and also give back to the others who helped build it by acknowledging their contributions.

4. Command respect; don't demand it. Yes, you have the title of president or CEO, or King of the Seven Seas, but that doesn't mean you have to act like a royal pain in the you know what. Get your team to respect and admire you by proving you care and that you have their back, even in

the smallest daily details. Many leaders aren't loved. But there is not one great leader who isn't respected—and respect has to be earned.

Aquaman leaders know the difference between being responsible and taking responsibility. They understand that taking responsibility entails being proactive. Passive complacency doesn't sit well with them, and it shouldn't with you either.

WHAT OTHERS HAD TO SAY

"Aquaman is one of the greatest characters at DC Comics and one of my favorites."

—GEOFF JOHNS, WRITER

"As we all know, Aquaman is somewhat the butt of the joke in the superhero world. There's something cool about that. I love the idea of being the underdog, coming in with a take on this underdog character and completely blowing people's expectations away. Like, 'Oh, you thought he was going to be a wimpy character? No no no.' It's going to be so cool."

—JAMES WAN, MOVIE DIRECTOR

"You know, it's cute and funny, I mean people make fun of him and there's a bunch of jokes about him. But I'm like 'Well . . . just wait. Let's just wait a little bit. And then we can make jokes . . .'"

—JASON MOMOA, ACTOR

"I spent 15 years trying to dig myself out of the Baywatch hole, and now I'm Aquaman. Life is very good."

—JASON MOMOA, ACTOR

"Aquaman has the ability to be a huge character, and I think we really brought him to a new level in comic books, and I'm hoping that new level continues to everything that is DC Entertainment. Certainly, that's the goal. He's one of our most recognizable and most important characters, and it's going to continue to stay that way."

—GEOFF JOHNS, WRITER

CHAPTER 13

THE IRON MAN
THE CHARISMATIC AND BOLD GENIUS

"Sometimes you gotta run before you can walk!"

—IRON MAN

CHARACTER BIO

I ron Man (Tony Stark) is a Marvel Comics creation. The character was born, like many other beloved superheroes, from the combined creative genius of then writer and editor Stan Lee and artists Don Heck and Jack Kirby. He made his first appearance in *Tales of Suspense* #39 (cover dated March 1963).

Tony Stark is an American billionaire playboy, business magnate, and ingenious engineer—or, as he says it himself in *The Avengers* movie: "Uh . . . genius, billionaire, playboy, philanthropist." As the story goes, Tony Stark suffered a severe chest injury during a kidnapping in which his captors attempt to force him to build a weapon of mass destruction. He instead creates a powered suit of armor to save his life and escape captivity. In the original comic, his kidnapper was a Vietnamese warlord named Wong Chu; but in our day, they are Muslim terrorists. The times, they are a changin'. Anyway, when he gets back to America after his ordeal, Stark enhances his suit with various weapons and other technological devices he designed through his company, Stark Industries. He then starts using the suit and subsequent versions to protect the world as Iron Man.

Iron Man possesses a wealth of powers through his powered armor suit. These powers include super strength, the ability to fly, durability, and a number of weapons. The primary weapons used by Iron Man are repulsor beams that are shot from the palms of his gauntlets. Stark initially tried to conceal his secret identity from the public, but that didn't last. He's proud of being Iron Man, and he wants the world to know it. In his beginnings, Iron Man was used by Marvel to explore Cold War themes, particularly the role of American technology and business in the fight against communism. In some ways, he was the poster boy of capitalism. Subsequent re-imaginings of Iron Man have transitioned from Cold War themes to contemporary concerns, such as corporate crime and terrorism. The hugely successful 2008 movie *Iron Man* has pretty much cemented his origin story for the public at large.

Throughout most of the character's publication history, Iron Man has been a founding member of the superhero team The Avengers and has been featured in several incarnations of his own various comic book series. Iron Man has been adapted for several animated TV shows and films. The character is portrayed by Robert Downey Jr. in the live action film *Iron Man* (2008), which was a critical and box office success. Downey, who received much acclaim for his performance, reprised the role in *The Incredible Hulk* (2008);

two Iron Man sequels, *Iron Man 2* (2010) and *Iron Man 3* (2013); *The Avengers* (2012); *Avengers: Age of Ultron* (2015); and *Captain America: Civil War* (2016). He will do so again in *Spider-Man: Homecoming* (2017) and both parts of *Avengers: Infinity War* (2018/2019) in the Marvel Cinematic Universe. (Wikipedia)

Robert Downey's performance as Iron Man is perhaps the most iconic ever for an actor playing a superhero on the big screen. He is Tony Stark/Iron Man personified—and we love him for it.

LEADERSHIP STYLE

While Iron Man has more of a coolness reputation than a leadership reputation, one cannot ignore his massive influence. *The Marvel Encyclopedia* introduces him this way: "Billionaire industrialist and philanthropist Tony Stark is perhaps the most influential superpowered individual on the planet. While Professor X has the respect of the Earth's mutant community, Stark's work as Iron Man, his long-term membership in The Avengers, and position as head of Stark International arguably gives him wider authority." As such, Iron Man is definitely a leader. Regardless of where you stand on his alcoholism and womanizing, or his stance on the Superhuman Registrations Act, which initiated Marvel's Civil War, Tony Stark did gather enough followers to prove his mettle as a great leader. Also, interestingly, the website ibtimes.com *(International Business Times)* released stats on the percentage of online conversations, ranking Avengers by popularity. Iron Man, with 16.7 percent, is second only to "Mr. Leadership," aka Captain America (18.7 percent). That, I think, says a lot about the pull, influence, and charisma of the character.

James Tarantin, author of *The Equation*, uttered the following gem during a speech:

> You have a choice, whether to be a madman or a bold genius. What's the difference? A madman is somebody who does the same action over and over and over for an unknown destiny. A bold genius is somebody who does the same action over and over and over again for a known destiny. That is why fortune always favors the bold.

While some of us, after reading this, inevitably realize we have been madmen at times, we also realize that Iron Man is a bold genius. This differentiation given by Tarantin is probably based on Einstein's well-known and oft-used definition of insanity: doing the same thing over and over again and expecting different results.

So now that we know bold geniuses are not madmen, what else could we learn about them? There are basically three steps bold geniuses take that ultimately lead to their greatness:

1. They come up with a great idea that can help many people and change the world.

2. They are bold about how far and wide they want to take this idea.

3. They never stop until they get there.

Tony Stark will work day in and day out on a revolutionary engineering project and go back to it, again and again and again until it has been perfected beyond human comprehension. He doesn't repeat his actions in vain. He has a known destiny, a very powerful "why." He is an expert at taking complex technology and making it fit in the palm of your hands.

While some would invent super-revolutionary fighter jets, Stark would take it further by shrinking the invention into tiny nanobots, all the while boosting cloaking technology and improving the weapons systems. That's very bold . . . and genius also. In that respect, Tony Stark is a cross between Albert Einstein and Richard Branson. That's why the character appeals to so many people. He is an inventive genius with a twist. When he fails, he fails forward and with style. Not everybody can pull that off. For one, when I fail, I just fail. I just haven't mastered the art of failing, so I suck at it. But enough about me.

Of course, Iron Man is fictional—very much so, I might add. Think about it: can you be super cool and charismatic and crush it in a science lab at the same time? That's a long stretch. Have you ever met a good looking and cocky jock, who is a super-genius, Einstein-type inventor at the same time? Neither have I. Now, I'm not saying they don't exist, I'm just saying I've never seen one. Nevertheless, there are men and women in our organizations who exhibit the dual prowess of being bold and genius without necessarily exhibiting the intellectual prowess of the Marvel character. You can still have genius ideas without creating engineering breakthroughs. There are hundreds of revolutionary entrepreneurs out there who prove their brilliance every day.

To put geniuses in context, here is what our friends at *Merriam-Webster* have to say on the word *genius*: "Exceptional intellectual or creative power or other natural ability. A person who is exceptionally intelligent or creative, either generally or in some particular respect." So genius can sometimes be just an idea, a concept, or a way of doing things that revolutionizes our world. Much of genius has to do with imagination. Albert Einstein said, "Imagination is more important than knowledge."

It's hard to classify which is greater in Tony Stark, his genius or his boldness. Whether in business or as Iron Man, he puts himself out there for the world to see. He is unique among superheroes: he wears his mask but wants everyone to know he's Iron Man. That's bold. While the others have a secret identity to protect themselves and their loved ones, he is proud to be who he is—come what may. He takes his chances.

In the first *Iron Man* movie, we witness his boldness as he decides to build his armor under the threat of potential execution in a cave. That's daring and gutsy. We also witness his boldness when he holds a press conference, first thing when he comes back to America, and announces to a shocked world that Stark Industries is pulling the plug on the weapons manufacturing division. Iron Man leaders have bold visions and make bold decisions. And when they make such decisions, it's kind of hard to argue with them since they are also proven geniuses. In many ways, their boldness is their genius, or as Johann Wolfgang Goethe said, "Whatever you can do or dream you can, begin it. Boldness has genius, magic, and power in it." Or, as bold genius Steve Jobs put it in one of his speeches, "Stay hungry; stay foolish."

STRENGTHS

Iron Man leaders' strengths are obvious for all to see. They are revolutionary leaders whose vision and ideas change our world. They are the makers of history. They have the ability to see and aim bigger than all of their peers. Their vision is phenomenally ambitious. All they see are solutions for everything. They never see the potential problems in their undertakings. To them, the glass is always half-full (in more ways than one, for Stark). This positive attitude serves them very well. Benjamin Franklin, Thomas Edison, Henry Ford, Albert Einstein, the Wright brothers, Nikola Tesla, and, more recently, Steve Jobs, Richard Branson, Jeff Bezos (Amazon founder), and Larry Page (Google founder) are all Iron Man leaders in their own right. And to that list, we can definitely add Stan Lee, who reinvented and revolutionized the comic book industry as we know it. All of them were world changers, bold geniuses.

WEAKNESSES

Stan Lee wanted to do with Iron Man what he had so successfully done with Spider-Man: create a character with obvious flaws that people would embrace. Mission accomplished. Tony Stark is a sanguine with all of the type's qualities—and all of its flaws. He is easily distracted, and he lacks some moral grounding and self-control. Women, booze, and partying have been his Achilles' heel, more often than not, in the comics and movies. Hence, it is quite understandable that he and Captain America ended up clashing in *Civil War*. Although they both live to serve and are two strong and decisive men, they are polar opposites in many ways. Cap is from the past; he is old school and conservative. Iron Man is focused on the future; he is progressive and liberal, bordering on the libertine.

Furthermore, Iron Man leaders are not always as thick-skinned as they seem. They can be quite sensitive and their genius can sometimes make them feel ostracized. Their huge undertakings also bring very heavy loads of stress on their shoulders. This can make them vulnerable to finding solace in a bottle of Vodka or other such addictive behaviors.

Also, they tend to be so focused on their passionate endeavors and projects that they neglect more important things, like their own health or family, for example. Weakness or not, I contend that they wouldn't change the world if they weren't as obsessed with their work and calling. I guess that's the price they choose to pay, and humanity is all the better for it.

EFFICIENCY RATING

When focused on his work, the Iron Man leader is absolutely fantastic. He is exceptionally creative, and his vision knows no bounds. He will envision projects others will think of as impossible and then pull them off with characteristic style. They thrive on success and are highly motivated. They don't change the course of mighty rivers, but they definitely change the course of history.

PEOPLE SKILLS: 8

SMARTS: 10

VISION: 10

CHARACTER: 6

ADAPTABILITY: 7

FOCUS: 8

"IT" FACTOR: 10

OVERALL: 8

CALL TO ACTION: GO BIG OR GO HOME

If, like me, you come from very humble beginnings, you might struggle with thinking big. "Go big or go home" might not be an expression that is part of your philosophy. When you are surrounded by working class family members, schoolmates, or a neighborhood where money is scarce, thinking big is not a natural inclination. It goes against the grain and tends to irritate your peers. But in order to be successful, it is a behavior that has to be learned. It is essential to impactful leadership and to a happy and fulfilled life. The higher the goal, the higher the possibility of significant achievement. We rarely hit a perfect mark on our goals, which is why it is important to aim high. If you fail, you might just fail a rung or two lower than what you set your mind on—but you will still be higher than you were. Les Brown, one of the world's foremost speakers, said, "Shoot for the moon; even if you miss, you will still be among the stars." But if you aim low, you will always hit your mark and achieve nothing worthwhile in the process.

> The higher the goal, the higher the possibility of significant achievement. We rarely hit a perfect mark on our goals, which is why it is important to aim high.

Tony Stark is a very bold entrepreneur and businessman. His greatest asset as a leader is how big he thinks. To him, there are no limits. He's always looking for the BBBB breakthrough (bigger, better, bolder, badder). He thinks very big and never limits his ambition or imagination. In fact, he thinks so big that his peers often think of him as not only bold, but an eccentric dreamer. If you're ambitious and have far-reaching goals and dreams, you can surely relate to this.

A very inspiring story about the magic of thinking big is the story of *Rocky*, written by Sylvester Stallone, a hero to many. "Sly" was a relative unknown to Hollywood in the mid-70s when he pitched his rags-to-riches script about an amateur boxer from the hood in Philly who becomes a world heavyweight contender in the fight of a lifetime. Rocky Balboa was his name.

Luckily, producers liked it. Unfortunately for Stallone, though, they didn't want him to star in it. But to Stallone, this was non-negotiable, so he held off on all the offers that didn't include him in the main role.

"They wanted every celebrated actor at the time," Stallone recalled once on the *Today* show. "And big-name directors, when they found out I wanted to be involved, they scattered, ran for the hills." Instead of Stallone, producers wanted Burt Reynolds or perhaps James Caan, who were big stars at the time. This was a big hurdle to overcome for the budding actor.

So at thirty years old, and with just $106 in his bank account, Stallone turned down a three-hundred-thousand-dollar offer—the equivalent of one million today—for the rights to Rocky. He was determined to make the film he wrote on his terms. He wouldn't budge on his decision to star in the movie as the protagonist. "It was really insane at the time 'cause I was pretty broke," he said of his decision to hold out. But, as we all know, it ultimately paid off—in a big way!

In 1976, *Rocky* won three Academy Awards, including Best Picture. Rocky and Stallone made cinematic history. He aimed for the moon and landed among the stars. You can too—if you have a genius idea and you're bold enough to see it through.

WHAT OTHERS HAD TO SAY

"He (Stan Lee) said he did it on a dare because back in the mid to late 60s there was a very strong anti-military industrial complex movement; it was a time of not trusting anyone over thirty. There were so many different revolutions going on. Stan also wanted a character that showed vulnerability. Stan said they got more female fan mail for Iron Man than any of their other characters."

—ROBERT DOWNEY JR., ON WHY STAN LEE CREATED IRON MAN

"I remember watching the Iron Man *cartoons when I was younger. I remember reading the origin stories and some of the Silver Age stuff, and I read* The Avengers—The Defenders *and then* The Avengers— *and that sort of brought me into Iron Man."*

—JON FAVREAU, DIRECTOR OF *IRON MAN*

"The similarity between Iron Man and Green Lantern is, unlike Superman or any of the X-Men or Spider-Man, anyone can be Green Lantern or Iron Man. All you need is the ring or the suit."

—MARC GUGGENHEIM, WRITER

"I think I gave myself a dare. It was the height of the Cold War. The readers, the young readers, if there was one thing they hated, it was war, it was the military. So I got a hero who represented that to the hundredth degree. He was a weapons manufacturer; he was providing weapons for the Army; he was rich; he was an industrialist. I thought it would be fun to take the kind of character that nobody would like, none of our readers would like, and shove him down their throats and make them like him . . . And he became very popular."

—STAN LEE, CREATOR OF *IRON MAN*

CHAPTER 14

THE OPTIMUS PRIME

THE WISE AND COMPASSIONATE FATHER FIGURE

"Freedom is the right of all sentient beings."

—OPTIMUS PRIME

CHARACTER BIO

O ptimus Prime has many different origin stories. The one I (and many others) grew up with comes from the television cartoon series from the 80s, or what is often referred to as "Generation 1." And since that's his first and best-known origin story by the original fans, we'll go with it.

Optimus Prime began his life quite humbly. His name was originally Orion Pax. Orion was a dock worker (or archivist, depending on continuity) during Cybertron's (the Transformer's home planet) golden age nine million years ago. At the time, a new breed of Transformers had recently appeared on the planet with new flight capabilities in robot mode. This made Orion idolize them. Unfortunately, when Megatron, the leader of these Transformers, approached him with inquiries about using one of the dock warehouses, Orion was swayed by him. Orion was then severely wounded when the cunning Megatron and his evil forces turned on him in order to claim the energy stored there. Alpha Trion, the wisest and most ancient Autobot at the time, used the injured robot as the first test subject for the new reconstruction process he had developed, rebuilding the frail Autobot frame into a battle-hardy configuration. With this reconstructive upgrade, Orion Pax became the legendary Optimus Prime. As the first of the Autobot warriors, Prime took on the mantle of leadership as the civil war against the newly coined Decepticons (Megatron's forces) erupted.

When the war on Cybertron depleted the planet of energy, Optimus Prime ordered the construction of a large ship and named it the *Ark*. With a crew of eighteen of his finest Autobots, Prime boarded the ship in the hope of scouring the galaxy to find another planet to thrive on. The Decepticons, led by Megatron, had also built a large ship, named the *Nemesis*. On board their own ship, they pursued the *Ark* and were able to intercept it on its maiden voyage. Using a tractor beam, they were able to board the Autobot ship while in space, and the ensuing battle onboard the ship damaged the *Ark*, which ended up crash landing on our primitive earth four million years ago with both factions on board—unconscious and deactivated.

In 1984, an earthquake reactivated both Autobots and Decepticons. They picked up where they left off and their war rages on to this day—on our turf.

LEADERSHIP STYLE

*"Effective leaders know that you first have to touch people's hearts
before you ask them for a hand."*

—JOHN MAXWELL

Optimus Prime has the amazing ability to connect with the hearts
of those he leads. They know he genuinely cares about them, and
that's why they're so willing to get their hands dirty for him. They
would follow him to hell and back if need be.

I grew up watching the exploits of the valiant and charismatic
Autobot leader on TV. I wasn't the only boy at the time to gain
much inspiration from Prime's unimpeachable morals and character.
I suppose saying he seemed larger than life to me would seem somewhat superfluous since he is, after all, thirty feet tall.

Optimus Prime is unique. He stands out because he is the only
non-organic leader in this book. He is also the only character not
belonging to DC or Marvel. I just couldn't leave him out of a book
about superhero leaders. Aside from Superman and Captain America, he is the most gifted leader in this book.

In *Transformers Universe*, a Marvel Comics publication in the late
80s, he is described this way:

If he had been on Earth, he would be a doctor, a mechan-
ic, a scientist and a warrior. But on Cybertron there is no
difference between these professions. So Optimus uses his
skills to heal and repair, which are the same things to Autobots, to improve the world around him and, if necessary, to
fight. Both in power and intelligence, he has no equal. He

has the personality of an Abraham Lincoln. He can be immensely kind, and his compassion extends to all that lives, including the creatures of Earth. Yet he will battle unceasingly to protect the weak and defend what he believes in.

There are no situations too dire for a Prime leader to handle. You'll never hear them exclaim in panic, "Oh no! What are we going to do?" Because of their many years of experience, pretty much all difficulties they encounter have this déjà vu feeling. They don't just know what to do, they remember what to do as well. They always see solutions instead of problems. They keep calm and speak authoritatively and decisively, no matter what.

Optimus Prime-type leaders are just amazing. They are very seasoned, and their wisdom and compassion have no equal. If you've had the privilege to work for such a gifted leader as a youth, you might have found yourself wishing he were your dad. Seriously. That's how special the experience of working for an Optimus Prime leader is. I wish I had that privilege.

STRENGTHS

Incredibly smart, strategically impeccable, with a scope of vision that sees very far ahead, Optimus Prime leaders are flawless when it comes to leading a team or organization on any project. They are expert delegators who know the strengths and weaknesses of all their team members. They are flexible and adaptable and can easily circumvent the inevitable bumps in the road. Their vast experience and wisdom is relied upon by their team who follows them without question. They inspire trust because of the amazing kindness and compassion they display—not to mention their track record.

WEAKNESSES

It has been said many times that Optimus Prime's only weakness is his compassion for others. Of course, in the corporate world, this translates to being vulnerable to shrewd or self-seeking back-stabbers. You know, the type that can be found in pretty much any organization? Most of the time, however, these leaders see them coming. No biggie, right?

EFFICIENCY RATING

This is one 'bot who shines! Prime leaders excel in pretty much everything. Their years of experience, combined with their intelligence, character, wisdom, and righteousness, are something to aspire to and emulate. And when they say, "Roll out!" people do it.

PEOPLE SKILLS: 10

SMARTS: 10

VISION: 10

CHARACTER: 10

ADAPTABILITY: 10

FOCUS: 9

"IT" FACTOR: 10

OVERALL: 10

CALL TO ACTION: BE WISE AND COMPASSIONATE

In *Transformers: The Movie* (1986), as a dying Optimus Prime is getting ready to pass on the Matrix of Leadership to Ultra Magnus, the following exchange takes place:

OPTIMUS PRIME: Ultra Magnus, it is to you, old friend, I shall pass the Matrix of Leadership as it was passed to me.

ULTRA MAGNUS: But Prime, I'm . . . I'm just a soldier. I . . . I'm not worthy.

OPTIMUS PRIME: Nor was I.

In this short sequence, we see Prime's humility shine through. He readily admits he wasn't always as capable as they (his soldiers) had come to know him. Ironhide, one of his oldest warriors and long-time friends, confirms this in Dreamwave's 2003 *More Than Meets the Eye* series. This multi-issue miniseries was a Transformers encyclopedia, which contained all the bios for all the Generation 1 characters. In the bio on Prime, we read what Ironhide says about him:

> He's got all the capabilities you'd want in a military com-
> mander: he's fearless, intelligent, compassionate, and pow-
> erful. But what I respect most about him is that he wasn't al-
> ways this way. I've seen him change and grow from a timid,
> unsure archivist who just happened to be put in charge, to
> a wise, confident leader. I think that's why every Autobot'll
> gladly follow Prime's lead without him even having to ask.
> He understands what it's like to be in their shoes—con-
> fused, scared oilless, and just trying to do what's right—so
> he'd never ask something of them that he wouldn't willingly
> do himself.

The good news in all of this is that Optimus Prime wasn't always wise, confident, and compassionate. He had to learn these
skills. He cultivated those qualities through a process. And here is

the good news: it's a lengthy process that we also can decide on as leaders. In fact, you should add it to your list of "shoulds." What better aim in your leadership journey than to be decisive in accumulating wisdom and to show more compassion? Of course, you don't just become wise and compassionate. You have to want it, and you have to do what it takes to get there.

"Wisdom is the applied synthesis of knowledge + experience + timing. It is the application of your knowledge and experience in the most potent way possible and in the timeliest of manners."

To be wise, you must study, understand, and love wisdom. But what is wisdom? Many people confuse wisdom with knowledge. The two are intertwined, but they are not the same. You cannot have wisdom without knowledge, but you can certainly have knowledge without wisdom. You see, wisdom is simply applied knowledge. The more knowledge you apply in your life, the wiser you are. The best definition of wisdom I could come up with goes, as follows: wisdom is the applied synthesis of knowledge + experience + timing. It is the application of your knowledge and experience in the most potent way possible and in the timeliest of manners. It's what you do with what you know that really counts—that's wisdom. A good leader always knows what to do with what he (or she) knows. Good leadership is applied knowledge towards a goal, which you will inspire others to embrace. Here are a few keys on acquiring wisdom:

★ Read good books, watch good videos/documentaries, attend good seminars/courses.

★ Read more good books.

★ Seek the company of wise men or women. Have them over for coffee, and while you're at it, take notes of everything they will tell you. Oh, and ask them which books they highly recommend.

★ Think. Yep, you need to be a thinker. You need to take time and reflect on each day. A day that was not re-flected upon is a wasted day because every day brings lessons. Deep reflection will give you hindsight and insight. And from those stem wisdom. You can even keep a journal to immortalize the process.

★ Model. I'm not a big fan of the "fake it till you make it" method. However, I once heard comic writer Neil Gaiman give the following advice in a speech, and I thought it to be, well, wise: "Be wise. Because the world needs more wisdom. And if you cannot be wise, pre-tend to be someone who is wise and then just behave like they would." Maybe, in this instance, a WWOPD (What would Optimus Prime do?) bracelet could come in handy as a reminder.

★ Ask for it. I don't know if you, dear reader, are a person of faith, but the world's bestselling book of all time tells us that, "If you need wisdom, ask our generous God, and he will give it to you. He will not rebuke you for asking" (James 1:5). Asking God, for me, has been the greatest source of wisdom of all. Therefore, I can-not omit it as I recommend where to acquire wisdom.

As for showing compassion, the golden rule is a very good place to start: do unto others as you would have them do unto you. There

is a touching story about the Civil War (not the one told by Marvel
Comics . . . the real one) that recounts the compassionate actions of
southern General, Robert E. Lee. I'll let this Union soldier who met
Robert E. Lee in the worst of circumstances tell his own story of
when he met Lee on the blood-drenched battlefield:

> I was at the battle of Gettysburg myself, and an incident oc-
> curred there which largely changed my views of the South-
> ern people. I had been a most bitter anti-South man, and
> fought and cursed the Confederates desperately. I could see
> nothing good in any of them. The last day of the fight I
> was badly wounded. A ball shattered my left leg. I lay on
> the ground not far from Cemetery Ridge, and as General
> Lee ordered his retreat he and his officers rode near me.
> As he came along I recognized him, and though faint from
> exposure and loss of blood, I raised up my hands, looked
> Lee in the face, and shouted as loud as I could, "Hurrah
> for the Union!" The general heard me, looked, stopped his
> horse, dismounted, and came toward me. I confess that I
> at first thought he meant to kill me. But as he came up, he
> looked down at me with such a sad expression upon his
> face that all fear left me, and I wondered what he was about.
> He extended his hand to me, and grasping mine firmly and
> looking right into my eyes, said, "My son, I hope you will
> soon be well."
>
> If I live a thousand years I shall never forget the expres-
> sion on General Lee's face. There he was, defeated, retiring
> from a field that had cost him and his cause almost their
> last hope, and yet he stopped to say words like those to a

wounded soldier of the opposition who had taunted him as he passed by! As soon as the general had left me, I cried myself to sleep there upon the bloody ground (*Memoirs of Robert E. Lee*, Col. A. L. Long).

That's compassion. That's an Optimus Prime leader in action. If you practice this on a daily basis, you will be well on your way to emulating Optimus Prime. You will be well on your way to being a great human being and a great leader.

WHAT OTHERS HAD TO SAY

"I auditioned like everybody else. I was told it was a hero, and I was told it was a truck. I was living with my brother Larry at the time. He had returned from service as a marine in Vietnam, and I told him one day I was going out to audition for a truck.

And he says, 'A truck?'

And I said, 'Yeah, but he's a hero truck.'

'This is really good, Pete, yeah,' he said . . . 'Well, if you're going to be a hero, be a real hero. Don't be a Hollywood stereotypical thing with the yelling and screaming.' He said, 'Be strong enough to be gentle.' And Larry was that way.

I had no idea what the script was going to be. But in effect, the lines just came out, and I just did my brother, Larry."

—PETER CULLEN, VOICE ACTOR, ON HIS AUDITION TO PLAY OPTIMUS PRIME

"To remove Optimus Prime, to physically remove Daddy from the family, that wasn't going to work. I told Hasbro and their lieutenants they would have to bring him back but they said no and had "great things planned." In other words they were going to create new more expensive toys."

—RON FRIEDMAN, WRITER, *TRANSFORMERS: THE MOVIE*

"It occurs to me that I really need a picture of Patrick Stewart as Captain Pickard driving Optimus Prime through space. I would follow either of them into the gates of hell without question or hesitation."

—BRIAN CLEVINGER, AUTHOR OF *WEBCOMIC 8-BIT THEATER*

THE STRUGGLE IS THE GLORY

★ ★ ★ ★ ★

"When there is no peril in the fight, there is no glory in the triumph."

—PIERRE CORNEILLE

Whether you are already a leader, aspire to lead, or are content with no leadership mantle or desires, life will bring your way its fair share of struggles and challenges. How we rise above them, our victories, gives us some measure of glory. Confucius said, "Our greatest glory is not in never falling, but in rising every time we fall."

Even if it goes unnoticed by anyone, our own personal triumphs over adversity make us grow and season us. They make us better. The struggles of life, our victories, our constant growth— these are what make our existence so flavorful, so glorious. Those among you who use the lessons from these cycles of adversity and victory to lead and bless others to their own victories have superhero leadership DNA. You not only are the hero of your own story, but the hero in other people's stories as well. You and humanity are all the better for it. You are fully alive and show glimpses of God's glory to your fellow man. You are what Saint Irenaeus was referring to when he said, "The glory of God is man fully alive."

Good leadership among men is found among those who embrace life fully. The greatest leaders, whether in comic books or in history, are those who not only embraced life, but also understood how sacred it is. It is from that blessed understanding that came their fortitude to lead and help others rise up. The greatest leaders are those who follow their bliss, fulfill their personal legend, and help others do the same on a daily basis.

> "The greatest leaders are those who follow their bliss, fulfill their personal legend, and help others do the same on a daily basis."

FIND YOUR INNER SUPERHERO

I hope you understand by now, as we reach the end of this book, that you are the hero of your own story. Your life and leadership will reflect how much of that truth you embrace. You can only lead as well as you think of yourself. Only the heroic will be able to truly help others in their struggles.

> "What you think about yourself will ultimately determine how, and if, you lead. What you think about others will determine how you will treat them and lead them. How you see the world will determine what you desire to bring to it."

Here are some inescapable truths: What you think about yourself will ultimately determine how, and if, you lead. What you think about others will determine how you will treat them and lead them. How you see the world will determine what you desire to bring to it.

Jaret Grossman, a motivational speaker, once gave an excellent illustration about this principle using the following story:

> Your brain is actually a circuit switch. Once you believe you are something, you actually embody it—you embody that feeling. If you were, God forbid, in a coma, and you woke up, and you didn't really have a memory, and you were told that you used to be a Navy Seal, and they want you back now, when you're healthy, do you think you would act differently and hold yourself differently, conduct yourself differently and have a different self-concept of who you are than if you were told you are a piano instructor?

And the answer to this rhetorical question is obviously a resounding YES! Always remember that if you really want to lead like a superhero, the most relentless supervillain you will ever have to defeat is your own inner negative thoughts about yourself. Here is what Dr. Maxwell Maltz, author of *Psycho-Cybernetics*, says about thoughts and beliefs: "Realizing that our actions, feelings, and behavior are the result of our own images and beliefs gives us the level that psychology has always needed for changing personality."

It's pretty simple really: when you change your thoughts, you change your life. Chances are, if you perceive yourself as a superhero, as someone who can really make a difference, you will exhibit those qualities. You will, when given the chance, help people in need.

I once heard Tony Robbins say in an interview that he used to always keep money in his wallet to be ready to hand it out to people he would meet who might need it. He went on to recall a time he did it, when he was absolutely flat broke in his early years. The story stirred something in me. I felt very inspired and began doing the same thing.

For the longest time, I kept a couple of twenty-dollar bills with me, just in case I met someone who might need it. One day, I was coming out of the bank, having just asked for a loan, of all things, and I saw a beggar sitting on the sidewalk. Right there, without thinking twice about it, I took out a twenty-dollar bill and handed it to him as I blessed him. You should have seen the man's eyes light up with surprise and gratitude! In all honesty, this small act of random generosity probably did me more good than it did him. I felt like a million bucks after this as I walked away—and all it took was twenty dollars.

Simon Sinek, the well-known leadership expert who wrote *Start With Why* and *Leaders Eat Last,* would explain it as the brain releasing endorphins, which give us that feel-good feeling when we do good. True enough. But all I knew was that I had made a difference. I felt good. I felt . . . like a superhero.

Leading like a superhero begins with being selfless—in the little things at first and later in the bigger things. We start small with little random acts of kindness: helping a neighbor to shovel snow, handing down money to someone in need with no expectation of getting it back, or just smiling kindly to people. The small things can make a big difference. If Superman is not above getting a cat down from a tree for a little girl, we shouldn't be either. Always remember the words of Ian MacLaren: "Be kind, for everyone you meet is fighting a hard battle."

EVERY HERO NEEDS A VILLAIN

"The more successful the villain, the more successful the picture."

—ALFRED HITCHCOCK

As a boy who grew up in the 80s, I became familiar with what is still considered today as the best decade for toys. It was great indeed. I was very big on He-Man and, later, was a Transformers fanatic. I always believed that the hero had no real purpose without a great villain. And there were great villains in our toy lines: Darth Vader in Star Wars; Cobra Commander, Destro, and Serpentor for G.I. Joe; Skeletor for He-Man and the Masters of the Universe; and the evil Megatron in Transformers. That's why I would always ask for the hero first, but ask for the villain as a gift later, for my birthday or such. Let's be honest here; we wouldn't see Optimus Prime shine without the likes of Megatron. Would Superman be as inspiring without Lex Luthor? And there would be no He-Man and the Masters of the Universe without the likes of Skeletor (and after school TV would have sucked growing up). And would Batman be Batman without the crazed Joker?

Yes, I did keep the best for last: the villains. You cannot lead like a superhero if you don't tussle with some supervillains. After all, a hero is only as good as his villains. And trust me, these villains we'll be looking at are so bad, they're goooood! Archenemies are what make the hero dig down deep into his own resources and rise to the occasion. They are the yin to the hero's yang; or is it the other way around? They challenge heroic leaders more than any circumstance ever would. One thing video games have taught me about life: if there are no obstacles or enemies in your path, you're going the wrong way. Or, as the saying goes, "For every level, there is another devil." And all these years, my mom thought I was wasting my time!

> ## "If there are no obstacles or enemies in your path, you're going the wrong way."

Of course, we don't have ghastly clowns or power-crazed billionaires or glider-flying goblins making our lives harder—well, at least I don't. But I live in Canada. We don't have as many freaks up here. No. But you and I have villains to face every day nonetheless. And do not underestimate them. These creepos can cripple you as badly as any super-powered freak ever could.

Let's consider the villains you will encounter as you strive to lead like a superhero.

The "I" Monster and His Acolytes

John Maxwell was once asked during a Q & A session at a conference: "What has been your greatest challenge as a leader?" To everyone's surprise he answered, "Leading me! That's always been my greatest challenge as a leader." And guess what? It will be yours and mine as well. Leading oneself is not only a daily challenge, but one that will last for a lifetime. While you will never master yourself completely, it should nevertheless be your aim. Lao Tzu, the Chinese philosopher of antiquity said, "Mastering others is strength; mastering yourself is true power." Another great man, this time Leonardo Da Vinci, said, "One can have no smaller or greater mastery than mastery of oneself." In short, you are your own worst supervillain. Your thoughts, your feelings, your beliefs, your emotions, master these, and the rest of your life should be smooth sailing. You, my friend, are most often what stands between you and your goals.

> *"Leading oneself is not only a daily challenge, but one that will last for a lifetime. While you will never master yourself completely, it should nevertheless be your aim."*

Your mind will often send two evil henchmen to trip you up. Their names are fear and excuses. One will paralyze you, and the other will try to justify your actions. In order to master yourself, you need to defeat these two posers. Or course, massive courageous action is the weapon of choice to crush them. When you push yourself through your fears and excuses, you demonstrate courage. It has been said many times, and it is worth repeating, that courage is not the absence of fear, but simply moving forward in spite of fear.

Nick Vujicik, the author of *Life Without Limits*, has mastered the art of leading like a superhero. The man has no arms, no legs . . . and no worries. Can you top that? This is why he is a true inspiration and a real-life superhero. Here is what he had to say about fear: "Fear is the biggest disability of all. It will paralyze you more than being in a wheelchair."

Remember, your mind has unlimited potential. Fear however, can hinder this potential severely. In that respect, your mind is similar to owning your very own Green Lantern Ring. Don't believe me? Here are more facts of how else it compares to the emerald warrior's weapon:

★ It is only limited by your imagination and willpower

★ It has a weakness against anything yellow. And yellow, as you well know, is the color which represents fear. Just like the ring, your mind's capacity is greatly diminished by fear (yellow).

★ It needs to be recharged every 24 hours. Basically, sleep acts as the charger for your mind to operate to full capacity.

And as for excuses, I like what George Washington Carver said: "Ninety-nine percent of the failures come from people who have the habit of making excuses."

When you really want something, you will find a way. But if you just kinda want it, you'll find an excuse. That's human nature. It's a protection mechanism that our mind has come up with in order to protect us from taking what it deems as unnecessary risks.

I have come up with a great mental image to determine if someone will move forward. Imagine in your mind a two-sided antique mercantile scale. I call it the action scale. It weighs your desire on one side and your fear on the other. Whichever weighs more on the action scale will determine if you make up an excuse or not. If your fear is higher, you'll make up an excuse. If your desire weighs more, you will move forward in spite of fear. You will take action.

I use the action scale on a daily basis to determine if my decisions are out of fear, or if I'm truly following my desires. It's a very helpful mental guide. You should weigh your every thought on it. I have found that if I am afraid of doing something, most of the time, it is an indication that I should do it, that blessings are attached to it.

Lazy Boy (or Girl)

*"Laziness is the secret ingredient that goes into failure.
But it's only kept a secret from the person who fails."*

—ROBERT HALF

People who fail often fail to see the part they played in being unsuccessful. It's often just a case of being lazy. You cannot be lazy and a leader. Period. Industry, blood, sweat, and tears are what will make you lead like a superhero. Slothfulness is not listed as one of the seven enemies of man (better known as the seven deadly sins) by the wizard Shazam (who gave Captain Marvel his powers) for nothing. Whatever your plans are as a leader, they will not work if you don't. And consider all the superheroes in this book: they are all very hard workers. Sometimes they go days without sleep in order to win. You have to defeat every ounce of laziness in your life if you are going to emulate them. Proverbs 12:24 says, "Work hard and become a leader; be lazy and become a slave."

"People who fail often fail to see the part they played in being unsuccessful."

Pride Demon

We've all heard that pride goes before the fall. History, and comics, have proven this to be true time and time again. One of my favorite characters in comics is DC's Black Adam. He is the archenemy of Captain Marvel in DC Comics, and he possesses the powers of the Egyptian gods: think Middle Eastern Superman with a nasty attitude. I'm just fascinated by this villain's character complexity. In the DC animated short entitled *The Return of Black Adam*, we see just how much damage pride can do to a man's character. During his fight with Captain Marvel, he says to him, while holding a woman by the neck:

Is this who you want to protect? Why? Because they are weak? When you crush an ant beneath your foot, do you feel remorse? No. Is this because you are evil or because you recognize yourself as a higher form of life? This is what the Wizard (Shazam) could not understand! If I have the powers of the gods, then am I not a god myself?

"Keep your pride in check because it does, indeed, go before the fall."

We learn from the comics that Black Adam was once a hero known as Mighty Adam, who used to help people in ancient Egypt. He was once their hero. So his is obviously a serious case of "power corrupts, absolute power corrupts absolutely." His heart was blackened by power and pride. Black Adam would certainly benefit from a chat with Spider-Man, perhaps he should post Spidey's famous "great responsibility" quote on his wall or something. But are we so different?

I admitted in the beginning of this book that if I had Superman's powers I would probably become a pro athlete. Now I don't consider myself to be evil. And I do think of myself as fairly humble. But I still have to admit that a degree of self-seeking temptation would definitely crawl into my soul if I were given such power. It would be daunting to remain "humble and kind" like Tim McGraw's song says. Of course, we'll never end up with superpowers, but sometimes just being given a promotion, title, or position can play havoc on our good intentions. Always remember that, and keep your pride in check because it does, indeed, go before the fall.

Mammon

I've often heard people ignorantly say, "Money is the root of all evil." That is a serious misquote. The actual quote is, instead: "The *love* of money is the root of all kinds of evil" (1 Tim. 6:10). Big difference. The Greek poet Anacreon said, "Cursed be he above all others who's enslaved by love of money. Money takes the place of brothers, money takes the place of parents, money brings us war and slaughter."

Consider the multimillionaires and billionaires in comic books (Bruce Wayne, Tony Stark, and Oliver Queen). They have proven, through their philanthropy, that they didn't fall for this grave fault. And don't make the mistake of equating success with making millions. I have known many very successful people who were well off, but didn't necessarily have millions. And I have seen some millionaires who, in my opinion, weren't very happy or fulfilled and, therefore, not successful. They don't always go hand in hand. The quest for success has undone many naïve souls through the love of money; they equated the two as one and the same. Grave mistake.

To avoid this pitfall, become a student of success, rather than a student of how to make money. Success, true success, spreads over the whole spectrum of life—not just our finances. True success will cover your health, mind, soul, family, and finances. And remember these sage words from a famous superhero: "No one can serve two masters; for either he will hate the one and love the other, or else he will be loyal to the one and despise the other. You cannot serve God and mammon" (Matt. 6:24, NKJV).

"Become a student of success, rather than a student of how to make money. Success, true success, spreads over the whole spectrum of life—not just our finances."

Miss Complacency

"Success breeds complacency. Complacency breeds failure. Only the paranoid survive."

—ANDY GROVE

Do not confuse complacency with laziness. Laziness is the lack of will to get going. Complacency is satisfaction with the way things are after you attained a level of success. Of course, there is nothing wrong with being satisfied with our results after we have put in effort on a life or business project. The problem lies in remaining satisfied with it. The above quote by Andy Grove, the Hungarian-born businessman, explains very well how to avoid complacency: be paranoid. What does this mean? It simply means to always be on the lookout for the BBD (i.e., the bigger better deal). Always have growth on your mind. Be very afraid of plateaus and be always on the lookout for complacency because it can creep up on you in subtle ways. Remember, growth is the essence of life. Therefore, we could say that stagnation (complacency), being the opposite, is the harbinger of death. You must slay it!

"Growth is the essence of life. Therefore, we could say that stagnation (complacency), being the opposite, is the harbinger of death."

The Negative Zone

The negative zone I'm talking about here is not quite the one from the Marvel Universe. No. I'm referring to negativity. Negative criticism, whether coming from others or yourself, is a no-no. Now I am not saying criticism is to be avoided altogether, but rather negative criticism—you know, the type of criticism that only brings you down and offers no suggestions, the type of opinion that stems from the insecurity and jealousy of others. If you have ever been in a leadership position, you've encountered it. Also, aside from what others might say behind your back or tell you to your face, remember you are your own worst enemy, and you might also tell yourself things that will bring you down. I have done this countless times. I have had many conversations with myself that went something like this: Who do you think you are? You can't pull this off. You don't have the experience or the credentials. You'll never make it.

I'm sure you've had similar conversations with yourself. This is "kryptonite thinking." Always remember: you don't have to put up with what you tell yourself. As soon as such thoughts manifest in your mind, you should put them in their place right away (i.e., the trash bin).

Or course, if you are leading, criticism in all its forms is unavoidable. It comes with the territory. The Greek philosopher Aristotle said, "There is only one way to avoid criticism: do nothing; say nothing; and be nothing."

Leaders take massive action and, therefore, submit themselves to massive criticism. In order to lead like a superhero, you will need to develop very thick skin. Invulnerability, like Superman, is not possible, so a thick, rock-like skin like The Thing is the next best thing. They key here, of course, is not to let negative criticism cripple you or cramp your style. You can't vanquish it, but you have to rise above it. And with experience and humility, you may one day even be able to learn from it. There are even leaders who look forward to it. These "tough cookies" relish it because, they reason, it's the only way they can truly improve and work on themselves. This, of course, although admirable, is not for everybody.

> "Leaders take massive action and, therefore, submit themselves to massive criticism. In order to lead like a superhero, you will need to develop very thick skin."

Egocentric Man

There is no room for ego or self-centeredness if you're going to lead like a superhero. Supervillains are self-centered. This trait belongs to them. Superheroes are selfless beings—most of the time anyway. They think of others first. Of course, as human beings, our first inclination is the opposite, so this requires a conscious and deliberate effort. Danish scientist and author Piet Hein has this to say about self-centeredness: "People are self-centred to a nauseous degree. They will keep on about themselves while I'm explaining me."

Indeed, we easily see others' faults, but we rarely see just how self-centered we really are. It's the proverbial plank in our own eye. We, as human beings, must be intentional about putting others' needs ahead of our own. This is hard. Sometimes it can be a superhuman effort to do so. But I have found that the more I value people, the easier this gets. The more I see their worth, the more I am inclined to serve them in a selfless way.

The cure for self-centeredness is found in our vision, in how we see people. I suppose we could say that self-centered people have "I" trouble and need their vision corrected. Self-centeredness shouldn't be found in any leader since it is a trait of immaturity, and leadership is all about maturity. The more we grow as leaders, the more mature we become, and the less self-centered we are.

> "The cure for self-centeredness is found in our vision, in how we see people. I suppose we could say that self-centered people have 'I' trouble and need their vision corrected."

Lady Malady

As trite as this sounds, poor health is one of the greatest villains for anyone who aims to lead like a superhero. If you are sick, sickly, or just plain overweight, you cannot operate at the same level of efficiency you would when fit and healthy. Your capacity as a leader can be greatly impeded if you're overweight or sick. This is one supervillain you cannot afford to underestimate. I'm talking from experience here. I have been TKO'd one too many times by dreaded ill health. Illness is unfortunate and can hit us at any time. This part of life's trials is hard to prevent. For all the other ailments, though, an ounce of prevention is worth a pound of cure. And yes, an apple a day is a simple way to avoid this dreaded enemy.

Moreover, have you noticed that superheroes are always in shape? They always have these perfect and muscular bodies. Of course, we can't all look like that, but the point is that we should exercise as much as we can. Your body is the temple in which your soul, your true self, dwells; you should, therefore, make it a priority to give this temple strong pillars (muscles). Jim Rohn said, "Take care of your body. It's the only place you've got to live."

I know this point is pretty basic, but you would be surprised to know how many leaders of businesses and organizations I have met who had poor health. I have witnessed some of them huff and puff and wheeze after only a short physical effort. On top of working in a sedentary office most of the day, many of them smoke or drink too much. I don't know about you, but I don't feel very inspired by that. And inspiring people is a key component of leading like a superhero. So take your health seriously. Leading takes a lot of energy, and you can only have high energy if you eat well and exercise.

> "Your body is the temple in which your soul, your true self, dwells; you should, therefore, make it a priority to give this temple strong pillars (muscles)."

The Legion of Haters

Of course, the list above is mostly about inner supervillains. Your life and mine will bring its share of outward ones as well—haters, as they are often called. There will be some people who are really out to get you. When people become hurt, self-centered, or self-serving, they can do some pretty nasty things. And unfortunately, we all encounter such people in the course of our lives. And yes, sometimes, unfortunately, we become the villain in someone else's life. We too can sometimes react poorly to pain. Nobody's perfect. However, we must make amends and ask for forgiveness once we realize it—and then move on.

Are there some people out there who are truly bent on hurting others, who are truly evil, who truly relish causing others pain? Yes, unfortunately, I believe there are. Sadly, there are some people who we are best to avoid. Darkness is a very real thing. I have seen it in the hearts of some. I am sure you have too. Like Alfred Pennyworth told Batman in *The Dark Knight,* "Some men aren't looking for anything logical, like money. They can't be bought, bullied, reasoned, or negotiated with. Some men just want to watch the world burn."

MIND YOUR VALUES

One morning at breakfast I was having a discussion with my seven-year-old son, Jason. I was a little worried about his heart. Don't get me wrong. He's basically a good kid and has a good conscience, but I was a bit concerned as to why he always preferred the villains over the heroes in his Star Wars Lego collection. I mean, all he talked about was battle droid this, Darth Vader that, Storm Trooper this, etc.

So, I asked him, "Son, do you know why heroes measure so much higher than villains?" I could see he wasn't following, so I added, "I know you perceive them as fairly equal because of what they can do in combat, their skills with a lightsaber are relatively the same. But superheroes are so much higher than supervillains because of their values. Heroes value the noble and good things in life: kindness, helping others, goodness, sacrifice, and life itself. Villains, on the other hand, value enslavement, themselves, conquest—even death! Always remember what you value. You value family, friends, kindness, nature, and good, clean fun. These things are very important, and they are what make you, and superheroes, so much better than villains."

As he left the conversation to go play before I could conclude, my wife rolled her eyes at me and said, "Nice try. Too bad you didn't use a language he would understand."

Okay, I admit I can sometimes be a little overly wordy with my children, but I really wanted to bring home the point that he needed to mind his values. As leaders, or aspiring leaders, the values we embrace make a world of difference. The components with which you choose to build your life and business philosophy are crucial to your success as a leader, even more so as a human being.

> **"Leadership is not something that should be pursued just to further one's career; it should be pursued because it makes one a better human being. The values and qualities it requires make it so."**

I don't put leadership solely in a corporate box. Since leadership is organic and vibrant, I believe it to be the sum of the best of human values. Leadership is not something that should be pursued just to further one's career; it should be pursued because it makes one a better human being. The values and qualities it requires make it so.

These values, which superheroes embrace, are prevalent throughout this book. Here are, in my opinion, the most important ones found among them. Make these a part of your "utility belt," and you'll not only have great values, but you will become invaluable to others:

INTEGRITY: Say what you'll do, and do what you say. Be a man or woman of your word. The word *integrity* is from Latin, *integritas*, and it means "whole." So be whole, not divided.

HONOR: A sense of honor is quite common among superheroes. Unfortunately, it is a dying value among us ordinary folks. The word *honorable* has to do with people and actions that are honest, fair, and worthy of respect. An honorable person is someone who believes in truth and doing the right thing—and tries to live up to those high principles. Captain America and Optimus Prime have a very high sense of honor.

SACRIFICE: *Merriam-Webster* says of *sacrifice*: the act of giving up something that you want to keep, especially in order to get or do something else or to help someone. That is, as we covered in the chapter on the Spider-Man leader, the essence of leadership.

VALOR: Much like courage, *valor* is defined as strength of mind or spirit that enables a person to encounter danger or challenges with firmness. It is another key component of impactful leadership. People don't follow cowards.

HUMILITY: I do not perceive humility as seeing yourself as necessarily inferior to others. Rather, it is the ability to see yourself objectively, to consider yourself and your contributions not too highly, nor too lowly, but just as what they are.

SELF-IMPROVEMENT: Always perceive yourself as an unfinished work, a masterpiece in the making. You can always get better. You can always do better. You can always become more and do more. Never be satisfied with your current state.

TEAMWORK: Leadership is teamwork. Like the popular sports adage says, "There is no 'I' in team." So be a team player and always recognize team members' accomplishments and contributions.

HEALTH AND WELLNESS OF SPIRIT, MIND, AND BODY: If health is not part of your values, you will eventually pay the price. And I'm talking whole health here: a sound body, mindset, life philosophy, and spirituality. These should all be cultivated. Neglecting these will result in a failing body, family, business, and/or relationships.

FAMILY: The superheroes covered in this book are people who highly value their families. Aquaman is a family man and had a son. Spidey loves Aunt May more than life itself. Superman cares deeply about his adoptive parents, Martha and Jonathan. Wonder Woman has the highest regard and respect for her mother, Hippolyta. Even Batman, who is somewhat cold and distant, would rather die than see anything happen to Alfred or his trainees.

If you are a leader in an organization and you don't lead your own family, you have misplaced priorities. Don't kid yourself; leadership begins at home and expands from there. I don't care what you've accomplished in the world. If you don't lead your family with at least as much concern as your job, you are failing as a leader. Lee Iacocca, the former CEO of Chrysler, observed the following: "Over the years, many executives have said to me with pride: 'Boy, I worked so hard last year that I didn't take any vacation.' I always feel like responding, 'You dummy. You mean to tell me you can take responsibility for an eighty-million-dollar project, and you can't plan two weeks out of the year to have some fun?'"

WHAT IS YOUR SUPERPOWER?

"A deep understanding of your own superpowers is a must before you begin reaching out to find other people to help you."

—KARL SAIB

In order to lead well and to surround yourself with an effective inner circle, you need to know yourself well and what you do best. In short, you need to know what your superpowers are in order to perform at your peak. Through the unique lens of looking at the different leadership styles of superheroes, you saw how uniquely qualified each of them is. That goes for all of us. We each bring something unique to the table. The key is figuring out what we bring and running with it.

I hope, through reading this book, you have gained more insight into who you are and how you can lead. How well you can lead will be determined by how well you can serve. And how you can serve will be determined by what your strengths, talents, and abilities are. In other words, you need to figure out what your superpowers are.

In *The New 52* Justice League, there is a running tagline throughout the early issues when the heroes first meet; they assess one another by asking each other, "So what can you do?" Green Lantern asks this of Batman and Aquaman. Superman asks this of Batman. Okay, they pretty much all ask Batman because they can't figure out what his powers are, and they are flabbergasted when they learn he's "just a guy in a bat suit." Let's just say his skill set is not as flashy as the others. And yet, he still manages to play a key leadership role among them. Why? Because he plays on his strengths. He knows what he excels at and sticks to it. Smart, Bats, real smart.

So, what are you best at? What defines you in your area of gift-edness? For each superhero, an evaluation of his or her leadership abilities was given. How would you rate yourself on a scale of one to ten in the following categories:

PEOPLE SKILLS

SMARTS

VISION

CHARACTER

FLEXIBILITY

FOCUS

"IT" FACTOR

OVERALL

Better yet, how would your inner circle rate you? Of course, not included here are your talents and abilities. You will have to assess those for yourself. Your leadership skill set is a great indication of what you can bring to your team, organization, or community. We do not inherit talents and abilities from God in vain. Your purpose is determined in large part by your unique superpowers: your gifts, talents, and abilities. Find them, and run with them. It will bless you and make you a blessing to others.

"Your purpose is determined in large part by your unique superpowers: your gifts, talents, and abilities. Find them, and run with them. It will bless you and make you a blessing to others."

PATIENCE THROUGH THE PROCESS

"Have patience with all things, but first of all with yourself."

—SAINT FRANCIS DE SALES

Learning to lead is a process that requires great patience, not only with others, but with yourself as well. Leadership is a destination, a journey. It is not an instant state of being. You don't shout, "Shazam!" and become a leader. But if you are intentional about it, you will steadily progress towards an ideal. As the saying goes, "A journey of a thousand miles begins with one step." So be intentional and begin. Like Zig Ziglar said, "You don't have to be great to start, but you have to start to be great."

Although I didn't mention it as part of the superhero leader's utility belt, patience is going to be your best friend on this journey. It will center you when dissatisfaction rears its ugly head. It will bring you peace during uncertain times on your journey. It will help you deal with difficulties and difficult people. Remember, leadership is a journey, a marathon—not a sprint. There is no such thing as a microwaveable leader. Leaders need to be simmered for a long time before they become tender-hearted, wise, and self-sacrificing. So be patient and be consistent. Like Ultra Magnus, Optimus Prime's second in command, says, "Consistency is victory."

"Leaders need to be simmered for a long time before they become tender-hearted, wise, and self-sacrificing. So be patient and be consistent."

ONE LAST CALL TO ACTION . . .

In all, it's really not complicated. If you want to lead like a superhero, you have to do what they do. Find the people in your community or organization who do lead like one, and model yourself after them. Hang out with such people. Read what they read; use your time the way they do. Obviously, as this book has shown, you can also model yourself after comic book heroes. Take mental notes when you see them act out leadership on the big or small screen or in comics. Be intentional about following the calls to action that make them strong and admirable leaders.

Be a super achiever like Superman.

Be a servant leader like Spider-Man.

Be disciplined like Batman.

Develop a strong character like Captain America.

Be decisive like Wonder Woman.

Be gritty and tech-savvy like Oracle.

Stand strong like Nick Fury.

Add value to people by valuing them like Professor X.

Be committed and responsible like Aquaman.

Go big or go home like Iron Man.

Be wise and compassionate like Optimus Prime.

"Model yourself after great men and women, but never imitate. Aspire to be and do like them, but never desire to be them. Be a student, not a follower. Achieve your own greatness through your own uniqueness. Be a leader."

If you take these calls to action to heart and apply them, there is no doubt in my mind that you will lead like a superhero, and you will make a difference in the lives of those around you. As you do, never forget this final call to action that will develop your own unique flavor as a leader: be yourself.

Never forget to preserve your own unique flavor. Always add to yourself in terms of character and skill improvement, but never lose your identity in the process. Model yourself after great men and women, but never imitate. Aspire to be and do like them, but never desire to be them. Be a student, not a follower. Achieve your own greatness through your own uniqueness. Be a leader.

"Blessed is he who has learned to admire but not envy, to follow but not imitate, to praise but not flatter, and to lead but not manipulate."

—WILLIAM ARTHUR WARD

EPILOGUE

I opened this book by fondly recalling how, as a four-year-old, seeing the first Superman movie back in 1978 really did make me believe a man could fly, just as their publicity campaign for the movie claimed. Of course, I grew up, and in doing so, I lost many childhood illusions. And yet, as I embraced my own hero's quest on this pilgrimage called life, I still held on to some dreams of greatness. As Paulo Coelho would say, I still believed I could fulfill my "personal legend." Superheroes still resonated with me as I found myself inspired by them . . . even as an adult.

This book was one of those dreams I held to so dearly. I held back from writing a book for twenty years prior to *Lead Like a Superhero*. Much of it was due to self-deprecating and limiting beliefs: How can a French Canadian write a successful book in English? How can I get published without a degree? I overcame this "kryptonite thinking" and began writing. The final result is one of my proudest achievements so far in life.

I believe that by striving to be the hero of our own story, we can develop into better leaders and, yes, even "fly" as a result. At the very least, we can soar higher as we aim for greater ideals and impart them to others. Nightwing put it this way: "You'll never know if you can fly, unless you take the risk of falling."

Leadership is all about making the jump, taking risks, and learning from your mistakes. It's about falling, dusting ourselves off, and getting back up again and again and again. Many of us, when we take that jump, realize we can fly after all. This is the best feeling in the world. Accomplishment is the seasoned leader or developing leader's greatest reward. I trust this book will inspire you to take more risks and develop into a better leader and a better human being.

> **"Leadership is all about making the jump, taking risks, and learning from your mistakes. It's about falling, dusting ourselves off, and getting back up again and again and again."**

May God (or "The Force," if you prefer) be with you as you strive to better yourself, lead yourself, and lead others like a super-hero. Take flight, and don't look back. Or, as a good friend of mine likes to say, "Up, up, and away!"

SUPER INSPIRATION

INSPIRATIONAL QUOTES FROM SUPERHEROES . . . AND SOME SUPERVILLAINS

"In my mind, one of the most famous pieces of comic dialogue is the oath sworn by Green Lantern. I gave this some deeper thought and realized that the oath is, in a way, applicable to real life. Anyone, should they choose, can swear an oath to stand against evil. Then it hit me. Have all comic heroes said things that are applicable in real life? Have they all said things that can inspire any of us, comic fan or not?"

—Adam Thompson
(graphic designer and creator of the *Heroic Words of Wisdom* series)

1. *"Why do we fall? So we can learn to pick ourselves back up."*
    —Thomas Wayne (Bruce Wayne's father)

2. *"You can take away my suits, you can take away my home, but there's one thing you can never take away from me. I am Iron Man."* –**Iron Man**

3. *"I believe there's a hero in all of us, that keeps us honest, gives us strength, makes us noble, and finally allows us to die with pride. Even though sometimes we have to be steady and give up the thing we want most. Even our dreams."* –**Aunt May**

4. *"If you make yourself more than just a man, if you devote yourself to an ideal and if they can't stop you, you become something else entirely—legend, Mr. Wayne."* –**Ra's al Ghul**

5. *"Doesn't matter what the press says. Doesn't matter what the politicians or the mobs say. Doesn't matter if the whole country decides that something wrong is something right. This nation was founded on one principle above all else: the requirement that we stand up for what we believe, no matter the odds or the consequences. When the mob and the press and the world tell you to move, your job is to plant yourself like a tree beside the river of truth, and tell the whole world, 'No, you move.'"* –**Captain America**

6. *"No matter how bad things get, something good is out there, over the horizon."* –**Green Lantern**

7. *"I had my eyes opened. I came to realize that I had more to offer this world than just making things that blow up."* –**Iron Man**

8. *"You're much stronger than you think you are. Trust me."* –**Superman**

9. *"There is a right and a wrong in the universe, and the distinctiois not hard to make."* –**Superman**

10. *"With great power, comes great responsibility."* –Spider-Man

11. *"I wear a mask, and that mask is not to hide who I am, but to create who I am."* –Batman

12. *"The answers you seek shall be yours, once I claim what is mine."* –Thor

13. *"If you cage the beast, the beast will get angry."* –Wolverine

14. *"This isn't freedom. We're holding a gun to every citizen's head and calling it security."* –Captain America

15. *"Life doesn't give us purpose. We give life purpose."* –The Flash

16. *"When you decide not to be afraid, you can find friends in super unexpected places."* –Ms. Marvel

17. *"The door is more than it appears. It separates who you are from who you can be. You do not have to walk through it."* –Franklin Richards

18. *"You only have your thoughts and dreams ahead of you. You are someone. You mean something."* –Batman

19. *"I shouldn't be alive . . . unless it was for a reason. I just finally know what I have to do. And I know in my heart that it's right."* –Iron Man

20. *"It's not who I am underneath, but what I do that defines me."* –Batman

21. *"Sometimes the truth isn't good enough. Sometimes people deserve more. Sometimes people deserve to have their faith rewarded."* –Batman

22. *"It's not dying that you need to be afraid of. It's not having lived in the first place."* –**Britt Reid (Green Hornet)**

23. *"Hold on to your dreams. The future is built on dreams. Hold on."* –**Optimus Prime**

24. *"Freedom is the right of all sentient beings."*
    –**Optimus Prime**

25. *"We have a saying, my people, 'Don't kill if you can wound, don't wound if you can subdue, don't subdue if you can pacify, and don't raise your hand at all until you've first extended it.'"*
    –**Wonder Woman**

26. *"Dreams save us. Dreams lift us up and transform us. And on my soul, I swear . . . until my dream of a world where dignity, honor, and justice becomes the reality we all share—I'll never stop fighting."* –**Superman**

27. *"A hero can be anyone. Even a man doing something as simple and reassuring as putting a coat around a young boy's shoulders to let him know that the world hadn't ended."* –**Bruce Wayne (Batman)**

28. *"Life is locomotion. If you're not moving, you're not living. But there comes a time when you've got to stop running away from things and you've got to start running towards something. You've got to forge ahead. Keep moving. Even if your path isn't lit, trust that you'll find your way."* –**Barry Allen (The Flash)**

29. *"It doesn't matter what the newspapers say or the politicians or the whole world. They don't define who you are. You do. And not by your words, but by your actions. The truth will come out. But until then, I'm going to keep fighting, just like you do."*
    –**Captain America**

30. *"There's an ancient wisdom I should have heeded long ago, if only I had recognized its truth applies as much to me as to all men. True happiness is found along a middle road. There lies the balance and the harmony—with reason and emotion, not at war, but hand in hand."* –**Aquaman**

31. *"This. This is what I am. This is who I am, come hell or high water. If I deny it, I deny everything I've ever done, everything I've ever fought for."* –**Green Arrow**

32. *"I want you to know that Mother may have given me life, but you taught me how to live. Love and respect. Your son, Damian"* –**Damian Wayne (letter to his dad, Bruce Wayne)**

33. *"There isn't much justice in this world. Perhaps that's why it is so satisfying to occasionally make some."* –**Martian Manhunter**

34. *"You'll never know if you can fly, unless you take the risk of falling."* –**Nightwing**

35. *"We are who we choose to be."* –**Green Goblin**

36. *"No one can win every battle. But no man should fall without a struggle!"* –**Peter Parker (Spider-Man)**

37. *"Always do your best. The rest is learning."* –**Superman**

38. *"I find the past such a worrying, anxious place. 'The Past Tense,' I suppose you'd call it."* –**The Joker**

39. *"President? Do you know how much power I'd have to give up to be president?"* –**Lex Luthor**

40. *"In any war, there are calms between storms. There will be days when we lose faith. Days when our allies turn against us . . . but the day will never come that we forsake this planet and its people."* –**Optimus Prime**

41. *"There's a thin line between being a hero and being a memory."*
    –Optimus Prime

42. *"Fate rarely calls upon us at a moment of our choosing."*
    –Optimus Prime

43. *"The greatest weakness of most humans is their hesitancy to tell others how they love them while they are alive."*
    –Optimus Prime

44. *"If you're good at something, never do it for free."*
    –The Joker

45. *"What if a child dreamed of becoming something other than what society had intended? What if a child aspired to something greater?"* **–Jor-El**

46. *"I have no idea where I'm going to be tomorrow, but I accept the fact that tomorrow will come. And I'm going to rise to meet it."* **–Donna Troy**

47. *"Masks. They hide our faces; they hide our fear."* **–Oracle**

48. *"In brightest day, in blackest night, no evil shall escape my sight. Let those who worship evil's might beware my power—Green Lantern's light!"* **–Green Lantern Oath**

49. *"You're going to make a difference. A lot of times it won't be huge; it won't be visible even. But it will matter just the same."*
    –Commissioner James Gordon

50. *"Someone once told me that the suit doesn't make the hero, so you fight it. You can be a hero. You just have to have faith in what you are and what you're gonna be. It's your choice, kid. You choose."* **–Booster Gold**

51. *"I have much to learn. I know that now."* –**Thor**

52. *"These are the years (teens) when a man changes into the man he's going to be for the rest of his life. Just be careful who you change into."* –**Ben Parker (Uncle Ben)**

53. *"There's only one God, ma'am, and I'm pretty sure He doesn't dress like that."* –**Captain America (referring to Loki)**

54. *"Legend tells us one thing, history another. But every now and then, we find something that belongs to both."* –**Nick Fury**

55. *"The future is worth it. All the pain. All the tears. The future is worth the fight."* –**Martian Manhunter**

56. *"You don't need to be a superhero to get the girl. The right girl will bring out the superhero in you."* –**Deadpool**

57. *"Whenever someone's asked what power they wish they had, flying is always at the top of the list. But I have to admit, I've learned to love falling too."* –**Nightwing**

58. *"Good is not a thing you are. It's a thing you do."* –**Ms. Marvel**

59. *"The training is nothing! The will is everything! The will to act."* –**Ra's al Ghul**

60. *"It's not being a hero. It's just doing the right thing."* –**The Flash**

61. *"My past is my own."* –**Natasha Romanov (Black Widow)**

62. *"Cats come when they feel like it, not when they're told."* –**Catwoman**

63. *"With its great gift, I can change human character; I can make bad men good and weak women strong."* **–Wonder Woman (on her magical lasso of truth)**

64. *"You don't always need a plan. Sometimes you just need to breathe, trust, let go, and see what happens."* **–Joker**

65. *"I've always done what I truly believed was right. At first, people called me a hero for it . . . and then a villain. As the memory of what I've done—and been—fades, I hope I will be seen . . . in a different light."* **–Hal Jordan (Green Lantern)**

66. *"The strength of this country isn't in buildings of brick and steel. It's in the hearts of those who have sworn to fight for its freedom."* **–Captain America**

67. *"Our ancestors called it magic, but you call it science. I come from a land where they are one and the same."* **–Thor**

68. *"I stayed in and studied like a good little nerd. And fifteen years later, I'm one of the greatest minds of the twenty-first century."* **–Mister Fantastic**

69. *"I'm loyal to nothing, General . . . except the Dream."* **–Captain America**

70. *"The greatest power on Earth is the magnificent power we all of us possess . . . the power of the human brain!"* **–Professor X**

ABOUT THE AUTHOR

Sebastien Richard was born in Montreal, Quebec, Canada, in 1974. He is a John Maxwell certified speaker, leadership coach, and trainer. He is also the author of the Kindle book *THRIVING ON PURPOSE: 8 Stepping Stones to a Successful and Fulfilled Life*. He currently resides with his wife, Elisabeth, and his three children (Jason, Marissa, and Katelyn) in Prince Edward Island, Canada.

My website:
https://thrivingonpurpose.com

Like me on *Facebook*:
https://www.facebook.com/thrivingpurpose/

Follow me on *Twitter*:
https://twitter.com/thiving_on

Read my blog here:
https://thrivingonpurpose.wordpress.com/

Don't forget to be heroic by leaving a review for this book on Amazon! Few dare to do so. Do you have it in you?

A free eBook edition is available with the purchase of this book.

To claim your free eBook edition:

1. Download the Shelfie app.
2. Write your name in upper case in the box.
3. Use the Shelfie app to submit a photo.
4. Download your eBook to any device.

Shelfie

A **free** eBook edition is available
with the purchase of this print book.

CLEARLY PRINT YOUR NAME ABOVE IN UPPER CASE

Instructions to claim your free eBook edition:
1. Download the Shelfie app for Android or iOS
2. Write your name in **UPPER CASE** above
3. Use the Shelfie app to submit a photo
4. Download your eBook to any device

Print & Digital Together Forever.

Snap a photo

Free eBook

Read anywhere

The Morgan James
Speakers Group

↗ www.TheMorganJamesSpeakersGroup.com

We connect Morgan James published
authors with live and online events
and audiences whom will benefit
from their expertise.